The Agile Manager's Guide To

MAKING
EFFECTIVE DECISIONS

The Agile Manager's Guide To

MAKING
EFFECTIVE DECISIONS

By David F. Folino

Velocity Business Publishing
Bristol, Vermont USA

Copyright © 1997 by Velocity Business Publishing, Inc.
All Rights Reserved
Printed in the United States of America
Library of Congress Catalog Card Number 97-61768
ISBN 0-9659193-7-4
Interior design by Andrea Gray
Title page illustration by Elayne Sears

If you'd like additional copies of this book or a catalog of books in the Agile Manager Series™, get in touch with us.

- **Write us at:**
  Velocity Business Publishing, Inc.
  15 Main Street
  Bristol, VT 05443 USA

- **Call us at:**
  1-888-805-8600 in North America (toll-free)
  1-802-453-6669 from all other countries

- **Fax us at:**
  1-802-453-2164

- **E-mail us at:**
  info@agilemanager.com

- **Visit our Web site at:**
  http://www.agilemanager.com

The Web site contains much of interest to business people—tips and techniques, business news, links to valuable sites, and downloadable versions of titles in the Agile Manager Series.

Call or write for a free, timesaving "extra-fast" edition of this book—or visit www.agilemanager.com/special.htm.

Contents

Other Books in the Agile Manager Series™:

Giving Great Presentations
Understanding Financial Statements
Motivating People
Leadership
Goal-Setting and Achievement
Delegating Work
Cutting Costs
Effective Performance Appraisals
Writing to Get Action
Hiring Excellence
Building and Leading Teams
Getting Organized

Introduction

We all make dozens of decisions each day. Some are everyday decisions, some more important, others of critical importance. For example:

Everyday: Which shirt to wear, how to get to work, where to eat lunch and what to have once you get there, whether to call a meeting on a certain issue, or how to arrange your office for the greatest efficiency.

More important: Which computer system to buy, which car to buy, whether to hire candidate A or candidate B, whether to file a lawsuit, when to launch a new product, whether to fire Mary, or how best to conduct research on a new market.

Of critical importance: Which strategy to pursue, what house to buy, whether to acquire a company or major piece of equipment, which product to develop first, whether to restructure a company or department, whether to take a new job, whether to move with the company to a new location, how to get money for growth (loan, equity, partnership?), or whether to install a new program like TQM or just-in-time inventory.

The consequences of decisions made in the everyday category

aren't great. And often, there's an answer that's either right or wrong. You wouldn't, after all, choose to eat the garlic soup when you have a meeting with the firm's largest client just after lunch.

But as decisions increase in importance, so do the consequences. If you fire Mary, will she sue? What if you pick the wrong computer system for your needs? What if you launch a product prematurely?

And when you get to decisions of the greatest importance, consequences can be enormous: If you pursue the wrong strategy, you may go out of business. If you choose to move to Wyoming with the company and things don't work out, it may take you a few years to put your life back together. If you switch to a just-in-time inventory system and implementing it takes twice as long as you thought it would, you may lose customers to competitors.

Worse, the more important the decision, the less clear-cut the answer. Any of five alternative decisions may work to varying degrees, for example. Or you realize that your best choice—after being watered down through compromise—has only a 70 percent chance of working.

Yet you can't run from making decisions. As Peter Drucker says, making decisions is "the specific executive task." Those who shy from decision making don't, in the long run, get far in their careers.

What You'll Learn

This book provides a framework for making decisions of all stripes, but especially those in the "important" and above categories. It'll help you do a better job picking the right computer system, house, machinery, job candidate, insurance policy, car, product or service, or strategy, to name a few.

In a nutshell, the process looks like this:

1. Categorize the decision to be made.
2. Identify the *real* problem.

3. Define the decision.
4. Generate potential solutions.
5. Evaluate the alternatives.
6. Decide and implement.

This framework may make it seem that decision making is a logical process in which you go from step 1 to step 2 without giving thought, yet, to steps 3 and 4. For some people, it is that logical. But in the real world, decision-making steps get mixed up. You'll start to think of alternative solutions while still formulating the decision to be made, for instance. You'll begin to evaluate alternative solutions as you come up with them. You may even hit on the right decision before you pinpoint the real problem.

The important thing is to be aware of all aspects of the process. Each step is a check on the others to make sure you are addressing the true nature of the situation at hand, and not one you or someone else thinks (or hopes) is the decision to be made.

The Benefits This Book Provides

No executive or manager has a perfect record in making decisions, but most of the good ones are right more often than wrong. This book will help you improve your batting average. You'll learn both analytical and intuitive techniques, you'll learn to appreciate the financial side of decision making (something that concerns your boss the most), and you'll learn to go about decision making systematically.

Having a good system is the only way to avoid the seat-of-the-pants decision making that so many of your colleagues practice—to the detriment of their careers. And having a system is the only known way to make fewer decisions. For with a good decision-making system, you get to the root cause of problems, rather than treating, over and over, symptoms.

The information here is provided in quick-read format. It

covers maximum ground in a minimum number of pages. You'll read the book in one or two sittings, then have it nearby whenever you need to make an important decision.

Best of all, you can put the tools, techniques, and methods outlined here to work *today*.

"An executive who makes many decisions is both lazy and ineffectual."

PETER F. DRUCKER
IN *THE EFFECTIVE EXECUTIVE*

Chapter One

*D*ecide to Avoid Problems

The Agile Manager, head of product development for a division of a large company, gazed out the strip of windows high on the wall of his office. He could see only the sky, and the branches and leaves of an elm, on the other side of the wall.

He liked it that way. If he could see people, he'd get distracted.

And now was not the time to be distracted. The Agile Manager's department was beginning to show signs of wear. People weren't as sharp, products not quite as cutting edge, and morale down slightly.

Nobody else saw these signs yet, he didn't think. There wasn't much to see. He couldn't even point to anything specific. Yet he had vague feelings that the shine was off the department. And it was his job, alone, to keep the sparks flying.

He knew he'd have to decide on how to improve things, and soon. But what, he wondered, was the root of the problem? I've got good people, good resources, good systems. They just don't seem to be in synch . . .

When a problem crops up, you know you need to make a decision. If an aging, cheap printer breaks down for the fifth time, you know it's time for a new one. You decide to junk it and buy another.

Many people, some experts included, seem to think decisions begin and end with problems that reach out and grab your attention. But the most effective managers know that good decisions, made early, eliminate problems.

Make good decisions now to avoid problems later.

Say you had decided years ago to invest instead in a high-quality, reliable printer, rather than a cheap one. Most likely, you wouldn't have had five breakdowns, nor the need to junk it and buy a new one. One good decision, long ago, would have saved you hours of frustration and additional expense.

That's why your goal, as a manager, is to make as few decisions as possible. Decisions made with foresight and care eliminate the need to make many more down the line.

When my partner and I started a business, for example, we decided that we would spend liberally for technology. We'd always buy the fastest computers and peripherals from reliable companies, and we'd spend to automate procedures whenever we could. That decision was not made in the face of any problems. Its sole purpose was to make us as productive as possible, keep overhead low, and save time and headaches.

Good Decision Makers: Not Hip-Shooters

An effective manager, in the eyes of the business press, is often a freewheeling, decisive person who hears the facts of a problem and shoots off a decision instantly.

Here's what former Chrysler CEO Lee Iaccoca has to say about that: "I'm sometimes described as a flamboyant leader and hip-shooter, a fly-by-the-seat-of-the-pants operator. But if that were true, I could never have been successful in business." Though Iaccoca believes good leaders are decisive, he also knows that good decisions aren't made rashly.

Hip-shooting decision makers often treat each problem as something unique. They solve a problem on the spot based on its superficial aspects. But many problems are symptoms of larger problems. And when you uncover the real problem, you can make a decision that eliminates scores of little problems that consume your time and energy.

Here's a simple example: A plant manager may find that a particular assembly line blows a circuit and shuts down about once a month. He gets it going again, then forgets all about it as he rushes off to douse another fire.

That blown circuit is a symptom of an underlying problem that, solved once, would keep the line going without a breakdown.

Good decision makers don't, therefore, usually come to quick conclusions. It takes time to dig out the real problem and evaluate alternatives. Good decision makers are patient.

Some managers can make good decisions quickly, even on the spur of the moment. But it's usually because they have years of hard-won experience and wisdom that help them get to the heart of a problem, and to its solution, quickly.

Decisions Made with Foresight

Some decisions are basic to the company's work. Once you make them, they either eliminate problems or make subsequent decisions easy.

Decisions on strategy are a good example. Imagine you're developing a new business and you have a choice. You can distribute your product through retail stores or directly to customers through the mail. You don't have the resources to do both, so

Best Tip

Don't come to a quick conclusion when making a decision. Dig for facts and ask for the insights of others.

you consider the ramifications of each alternative. After careful analysis, you decide to market directly to consumers.

A decision of that magnitude allows you to narrow your focus to the work at hand: developing direct marketing pieces for the mail, creating space advertisements, and putting in systems to handle orders, among other things.

So when a distributor calls you to inquire about taking on your line of goods, you don't have to think twice. The answer is no. You sell through the mail only.

To make decisions with foresight, have a clear-cut:

- Mission for your company or department
- Overall strategy in support of the mission
- Goal for each operation
- Understanding of your success factors or advantages in the marketplace (like superior quality, great customer service, or speed)
- Understanding of how technology is changing your business
- Knowledge of regulations and laws that affect you
- Knowledge of your strengths and weaknesses, and those of competitors
- Understanding of where your industry is headed.

Bill Gates and his crew at Microsoft, in a rare turnabout, decided to change Microsoft's focus to the Internet. He stopped projects midstream, redeployed people, and went on a buying binge in pursuit of companies he felt were ahead of Microsoft in Internet knowledge and products.

Time will tell whether Gates made the right decision, but in making it he left everyone at the company clear about the company's strategy. That both eliminated problems and made subsequent decisions easier.

Opportunities for Productive Change

As the Microsoft example shows, good managers are forever scanning the business horizon. Decisions made in response to changes, they know, keep the organization on course and healthy.

Fertile grounds for capitalizing on change include:

- Technology
- Market tastes and trends
- Government policy
- Demographics
- Revolutions in any value-chain area (like just-in-time inventory replenishment or marketing via the Internet)
- New ideas in structuring organizations.

Faced with changes in these areas, making a decision to refocus the company can be wise. If you do a good job thinking ahead, you can eliminate potential problems like sinking sales or profits, low morale, obsolete products and services, inefficient organizational structures, and outdated business practices and processes.

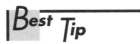

Best Tip

Never forget: Business should be simple. Beware those who complicate or fog up decision making unnecessarily.

Though often done in a ham-fisted way, restructurings and downsizings are appropriate responses to huge changes in markets, especially globalization, and the rise of the superefficient organization. A little bloodletting now can eliminate major problems, some of them potentially fatal, in the future.

Business Should Be Simple

People complicate the businesses they are involved in, which leads to the making of many decisions. Kenichi Ohmae, legendary Japanese strategist, puts your purpose as a decision maker in perspective. Every successful business has just a few of what he calls "key factors for success." These may reside in your product, marketing, distribution, or any other area of the value chain. When you know your key factors for success, decision making is easier.

Ohmae mentions, for example, that a key factor of success for banks has always remained the same: Get as much money as you can, as cheaply as you can, and lend it out at the highest rate the market will bear.

If bankers remembered this, it would be easy for them to decide not to get into complicated, risky development deals or enter new areas like the securities industry.

Create Problems

Good decision makers "create problems"—and the need for new, high-level decisions—through their management styles. Created problems are far better than those that slap you on the back hard.

Here's an example: A manager decides that her department should be 10 percent more productive. That decision creates a useful problem: How are we going to meet the goal?

Likewise, a visionary head of a start-up creates problems. She feels she can see the future, and her company in that future owns 90 percent of a market not yet invented. How is the company going to create the market? How is it going to maintain control over it?

Problems, indeed—but productive ones that keep people focused and companies humming.

The Agile Manager's Checklist

✔ Understand that while many decisions begin with the onset of a problem, the best ones eliminate problems.

✔ To keep your organization productive, make decisions in anticipation of changes in technology, market trends, regulation, and demographics.

✔ "Create" problems occasionally to increase your area's efficiency and preparedness.

Chapter Two

Categorize the Decision

The Agile Manager had just confided in Wanda, his second-in-command. "Does this make sense to you?"

"Now that you mention it, yes. Anita and William seem to be at each other's throats, and neither of the last three products did quite as well as we hoped. And I don't hear as much laughter in the hallways. Nope, it's not like it was a year ago. Good for you for figuring this out."

"But," began the Agile Manager, "I haven't figured anything out. I see symptoms of a problem without knowing what the problem is."

"Well, I can tell you I don't think it's a problem with our goals or our strategy. Sure, the products haven't done spectacularly, but nobody in the medical field is doing that well. Even Murphy Technology seems to be in a slump. Yet our products continue to be standards for hospitals and labs."

"And I don't think it's a people problem," added the Agile Manager. "William and Anita like each other. They just seem to be getting into each other's way."

Wanda snapped upright. "Hey—you're right. And Manuel and Nancy are in each other's way, too. Yesterday I saw them fighting over who would get to use the new analyzer. Maybe," she said

with a glimmer in her eye, "we have some kind of organizational problem. Maybe we need to rejigger things in the department."
"Rejigger?" said the Agile Manager, arching an eyebrow.
"Yeah—rethink how people work together. Who works with whom, where people are located, how we sequence activities— that kind of thing."
"Hmm," said the Agile Manager, stroking his chin. "An operations problem. You may have something. But if you're right, then what?"

The last chapter suggested that the perfect manager anticipates problems and makes decisions that skillfully heads them off. Alternatively, the perfect manager makes decisions that create productive problems.

None of us—great decision makers included—is perfect. We can't pay attention to everything. Unanticipated problems, therefore, tip us off that a decision has to be made about an issue that may have crept up on us.

What Kind of Problem Is It?

When faced with a problem, keep Peter Drucker's dictum in mind: Make a decision only when the situation will deteriorate if you don't. In other words, don't waste your time.

It's time to make a decision if a situation will worsen if you don't do anything.

When you have a problem that won't wait, first categorize it. Categorizing problems helps you size them up. You'll begin to see how deep they are and how long they'll take to solve.

Problems can be one of several types:

Factual. Factual problems have answers that are right or wrong. You can usually solve them quickly. For example, how do you set up a 401(k) plan? How do you make the new photocopier work properly? What time is the next sales meeting? With such problems, you need only decide to find the right answer.

Operational. These problems have to do with systems, work processes or practices, and technology. It's a good bet that operational problems, especially recurring ones, have deep roots. After getting to the bottom of the problem, you'll need to solve it once and for all.

Tactical. Tactical problems are those in areas that support your goals. Say your company's overall goal for this year is to increase sales 10 percent. You are using a number of tactics to meet that goal, like increasing your marketing budget, putting a few more people on the road, and improv-

Best Tip

Categorize decisions and gauge their urgency. Doing so will help you know where to begin.

ing customer service. One or more of your tactics, however, aren't paying off. Why isn't the tactic working? Should you scrap it? Revamp it? Reconfigure it?

Tactical problems are knotty and often require a good deal of analysis that leads to a decision that solves the problem.

Strategic. Strategic problems involve decisions of the highest order. They are about your organization's broadest goals. Poor strategic decisions put your very business at risk.

Symptoms of strategic problems may be falling sales or profits, low morale, inefficient processes or systems, or competitors eclipsing you in any number of ways. You need to make one or more decisions to change the company's course.

The Microsoft example in the last chapter is an example of a strategic problem. Gates and his senior managers clearly decided that the Internet would have a profound impact on all citizens in technologically advanced countries. He needed to reset Microsoft's course to capitalize on the opportunity.

Other strategic decisions include which products or services to produce, how to divide resources among departments, which markets to enter, whether to restructure, which countries to sell in, or what overall marketing strategy to pursue.

People. Managers, it's safe to say, have more problems with people than with anything else. And people problems always involve decisions: Should I hire Jim? Fire Joan? Move Ron into a new area? Restructure Rosie's job? Give Tim a warning? Give Tammy different tasks? Promote Frannie into the new position?

People problems, though common, are often easy and quick to solve. That's because you've probably already done the research required—you know the people involved and their strengths and weaknesses. And usually you know, at an intuitive level, the proper solution.

So what keeps you from deciding? In no other area can you see the impact of your decision so quickly, and that's scary. If you fire Joan, for instance, she'll provide feedback on your decision instantly.

Why categorize a problem? It's the first chance you have to get a conceptual "handle" on it. That enables you to begin to understand it and its scope, and what to do about it.

There's No Right or Wrong

Note that in all but the first category (factual), decisions usually aren't right or wrong. More than one alternative may work, for example, or the results of any may be (and probably are) unclear. The higher level the problem, the murkier things get.

Even decisions that seem cut and dried to an outsider are fuzzy to those making the decision. If a product's sales are poor, for example, you should kill it, right? Maybe not. Increasing the marketing budget or focusing on one distribution channel could revive it. Killing the product is but one choice of many.

Gauge Urgency

After categorizing your problem, ask yourself: How urgent is it? If a situation is flying out of control, stabilize it. Then assess the urgency of the problem.

In the case of a broken piece of equipment, you may need to devote the next twelve hours to it. If it's a rare-but-recurring glitch in a software program, you can work on the problem at a more leisurely pace. In general, the more time you can take, the better. You'll understand the problem better, and experience and wisdom will come into play via your intuition.

Size Up the Problem

Some problems aren't worth spending much time on. Give easy problems to lower-level people to handle, or take two minutes and handle it yourself. But never forget that lots of little problems may hide a big one.

Say, for example, you find yourself expediting late orders once a week. It's easy to go into the shipping department and say, "Make sure this order gets out today." But why do you have a problem that recurs? Is there a flaw in the fulfillment system? A

> **Best Tip**
>
> Some problems aren't worth your time. Give a problem to the lowest-level person who can handle it.

poor employee? A process in need of reengineering? The frequent problem signals a deeper disorder. Take the time to find out what it is.

Push Problems Downward

Generally, push problems down to the lowest level possible. If you can, make problem solving a responsibility for anyone on the staff. Then, when people bring a problem to you, they'll bring a solution as well.

If employees at lower levels are handling lots of problems, however, you're not doing your job. We've all heard stories of customer service people who go to extraordinary lengths to please the buyers of your products or services. But such stories should be an exceptional event. Your processes should be smartly organized and well oiled, making heroics unnecessary.

Assume Problems Require Deeper Analysis

When investigating a problem, your first thought should be, "This is most likely a symptom of something larger. What is the larger problem?"

That approach encourages you to dig deeper to find the problem and make a decision—often resulting in a rule or procedure—that eliminates problems of that nature.

This doesn't mean you start to work building up a rule book to cover all contingencies. That approach has been tried, and the ultimate end, for AT&T, was a set of policy manuals that occupied a wall-length bookshelf.

Rather, you're uncovering principles of good management that guide you and your employees in productive practices.

I remember, as a newcomer to the publishing industry, facing problem after problem with printing companies. For a while I had fun. I learned a lot and felt vital to the company. Then, in a blinding flash of the obvious, I realized, "Every time I spend an hour fixing this problem or that, I'm not working on the products that earn my salary. I should be figuring out how to avoid problems, not immersing myself in them."

Best Tip

Always assume that the problem you encounter is merely a symptom of something deeper that requires a decision.

That thought led to a principle known to anyone who dealt with printers in pre-desktop publishing days: Always give the printer more information than you think is necessary about how you want a finished publication to look.

Putting that principle into practice cut in half the number of problems I faced.

Sometimes a Sound Decision: Do Nothing

Time is an ingredient in all decisions, and sometimes it's the most important one. I can't tell you how often good decision makers have said to me, "Sometimes I leave a problem alone for a while. Frequently it goes away before I have to decide."

Doing nothing is thus a decision in itself, and it may be the right one. By waiting, a new piece of information occasionally pops up that changes your plans. (Doing nothing is not an alternative, however, if you put off a decision because you fear the consequences.)

When the World Wide Web was just starting to take off, I built a nice Web site for the company I worked for. I desperately wanted our customers to visit the site; I felt it had a lot to offer and would cement their loyalty to us. Customers, however, stayed away in droves.

> ## *Best Tip*
>
> Doing nothing is in itself a decision. But make sure it's a conscious choice, and not the result of neglect or fear.

I figured, correctly, that the main problem was one of access. Most people at that time weren't hooked up to the Internet, and they didn't know how to get connected. (It was before America On-Line and others provided access to the Web.) Goaded on by a business acquaintance with the right hardware, I came up with a scheme in which the company I worked for would become an Internet access provider. We'd offer our subscribers access, get them to our Web site, and make money to boot.

I pushed for a decision, but a wiser mind than mine counseled me to wait. Within six months (literally), Internet access providers numbered in the thousands. Solving our problem of low traffic by providing access ourselves would have been a costly disaster.

All this is obvious in hindsight. But at the time, the situation was muddy. Time clarified it.

Another reason to go slowly is that any decision has an impact. To borrow a term from medicine, making a decision is "invasive." Offering our customers Internet access, for instance, would have required a new set of systems and procedures, and an increased workload for our customer-service people.

That's why Peter Drucker likens decision making to surgery. Just as you don't have surgery unless it's absolutely necessary, you don't make decisions that don't need to be made.

The Agile Manager's Checklist

✔ Know the different kinds of problems:
- Factual, which have answers that are right or wrong.
- Operational, which have to do with systems and practices.
- Tactical, having to do with the maneuvers you're employing to reach goals.
- Strategic, which have to do with your organization's broadest goals.
- People.

✔ Stabilize urgent problems, then take your time in solving them.

✔ Assume problems have deep roots.

Chapter Three

Identify the Real Problem

"Manuel," asked the Agile Manager, "how's the new analyzer working out?"

"It's beautiful. It's a piece of art. I wish all our products were as elegant. It saves me at least a couple of hours on each project, and it provides feedback that gives me ideas on other things."

Like what, wondered the Agile Manager. I'm intrigued. Instead he asked, "How does everyone else like it?"

"Too well! We fight over it. Hey—how about buying another one? We'd put it to good use. It would save time."

The Agile Manager ignored the question. "Is there any other equipment you fight over?"

"Oh, yeah. The CAD workstation, for one thing. And we even fight over the large table—you know, the one where we can spread out all our work. It's silly sometimes. Just last week Nancy wanted to . . ."

*   *   *

". . . and William and Phil were shouting at each other?" The Agile Manager looked at her with disbelief.

"Well, yes," said Anita, not wanting to say much more. "But they tried to hide it, pretending to be buddies once they came out

27

of the room. And they've been fine ever since."

And the third party in this ménage à trois, thought the Agile Manager, is that damn circuit analyzer. Maybe Manuel is right, maybe we need another one. "What do you think the real problem is?" he asked.

"You really want to know?" Anita asked. He nodded. "I think maybe we're all too independent. If we had to work more closely together—if we shared more jobs—we'd make better use of the resources we have here."

Better, thought the Agile Manager. Now we're getting somewhere. "Tell me more," he said to Anita.

A problem usually signifies that a decision must be made. But don't rush to solve a problem, declare victory, and walk away. Take enough time to identify the real problem.

Superficial Solutions Are No Solution

Let's say your department is swamped with work. The solution seems obvious. You need another employee. So you hire the employee, which lightens the load—for six months. Then you're back where you were, knee deep in paper, and on top of that, you have higher costs.

Any problem is usually a symptom of something deeper, and a quick fix, like hiring another body or acquiring another machine, may not address the real situation.

The problem in this example lies elsewhere. It could be in the way your department processes work. It may be a couple of bad employees who foul up the system. It may be aging technology. It may be how work is done elsewhere in the company.

Best Tip

A "quick fix" usually will not address the real problem. Take the time to find out what it is.

Another example: Company profitability is down. You feel you know the reason—your two biggest suppliers raised prices.

You've shopped around for cheaper materials and found a new supplier who will sell material a nickel cheaper on the dollar.

That's another superficial solution that barely addresses a problem that's bound to recur. Too bad, because you have an opportunity.

The opportunity lies in thinking differently about how you accomplish work. Maybe you can substitute cheaper, better material at a lower cost. Maybe you can alter the processes by which you do work.

Best Tip

Form an opinion as to the nature of the problem, but then treat it as a hypothesis that must be tested.

Doing either may result in new advantages over competitors and breathe new life into your products and workforce. Problems of this sort are springboards for innovation.

Start with an Opinion

As Peter Drucker points out, it's impossible to do what most experts say to do when faced with a decision to make: Start with an unbiased, blank mind; gather facts; draw conclusions; decide.

Why is it impossible? Humans, by nature, start with an opinion and fit the facts they find to it. We can't be truly objective.

Knowing that, understand that any conclusion that you come up with regarding a problem should be treated as a working hypothesis that you'll need to test. When you gather information about the problem, be aware of your biases and look for reasons that refute your hunch.

Gather Information

How can you get to the root of the problem to enable you to begin working on a decision that eliminates it? There's no recipe, mainly because decisions run the gamut from mundane to monumental. And every situation is vastly different. Nonetheless, here are a few ideas that will help you uncover the real problem and begin to formulate a framework for making a decision:

Look beyond the "obvious" solution. A company's loading docks were always jammed, causing problems both for the company and those transporting goods to and from it. The obvious solution was to expand docking space, either by adding new space or finding a new warehouse altogether.

A few people in the company looked at the problem from a different angle. "How could we solve it," they asked, "without going to the expense of expanding space?" They solved the problem by restructuring traffic flow—how and where truckers pulled up to the building.

Put the problem in question form. For example:

- How can we get people to come in on time?
- How can we stop shipping orders to the wrong address?
- How can we improve sales in the Dakota region?
- How can we streamline the department to improve productivity?
- How can we keep the assembly line running at optimum speed without shutdowns?

Putting problems in question form can help you get beyond the symptom you're faced with. If Joe, Ginny, and José habitually come in late, asking a broad question helps you get beyond their personalities and how they annoy you. Maybe you'll see that each has children and needs a slightly more flexible schedule than the rest. A new policy—not disciplinary action—may be the answer.

Talk to those closest to the problem. They understand it best. Ask what they think the root cause is. Gather opinions.

This is essential. I once oversaw a production department in which there were many problems with compatibility among machines. It was only by interviewing, in depth, the people who operated the machinery that we could begin to understand, let alone solve, the problem.

Listen. Just because you're a manager, don't pretend you have all the answers. Everyone knows you don't. Listen carefully to opinions and dig for details.

Look for cause and effect. Maybe every time Paul works on machine A, quality goes down. Or productivity is off on Monday mornings in the fall, mainly because of the football pool. Or your customer-service staff is battling the new order-entry software because people didn't receive enough training.

Take it to a higher level. A machine breaks down repeatedly. Look to the overall system to which it's connected—power sources, other machines, entire processes.

If you feel you need to hire another person, first ask, "How can we accomplish our work better?" The answer may be something other than hiring. It may even lead to the question, "Should we even be doing this work at all?"

Best Tip

Always gather the insights of those closest to the problem. They may understand it best—if not have a solution already.

Get reactions to your opinion. "Charlie," you say. "I suspect the root of this problem is in the software we use to fulfill orders. It's got a couple of glitches that recur in a pattern. Here's what I'm thinking . . ." Charlie, being human, will be all too glad to tell you what he thinks of your idea. Be grateful if he says something like, "I had a computer consultant go over that code line by line. She couldn't find a thing. But you know what I'm thinking? Bill is always on duty when the foul-ups happen . . ." Maybe you're both wrong, but at least you've expanded the possibilities.

Ask "Why?" three times in a row. This is another way to get beneath symptoms to a problem. "Why does the fuse blow? Because the circuit gets overloaded. Why does the circuit get overloaded? Because we have too many machines hooked up to it. Why do we have too many machines hooked up to it? Because we've been growing too fast to take the time to think about the infrastructure for accomplishing work." Bingo.

Get multiple points of view. Talk to anyone remotely connected with the situation—even people in other parts of the organization and those outside the company, like vendors or customers.

Where do you stand vs. your competitors? The *Annual Statement Studies* from Robert Morris Associates can tell you. Find it at any good research library.

Assess rules and policies. Maybe you're inundated with paper and it's keeping you and your people from doing work. You pick up a rather worthless report that lands on your desk each Wednesday and ask, "Why do I get this?" Maybe it turns out the person who held your job in 1988 decided it would be worthwhile to read. If it was then, you think, it's not now. Agitate for a companywide decision on reports and other paper clogging the office.

Compare your problem with others. Here's where experience helps. What's the problem like? You may have met it before in different clothes.

Compare your financial indicators with those of other companies. Say profitability is down. What's average profitability for companies in your industry? What's the average return on equity? What are typical averages for expenses? If you don't know the answers to these questions, a great resource is the Robert Morris Associates *Annual Statement Studies*. It lists financial data, including ratios, for companies of various sizes in all industries. You can usually find it at a large public or university library, or call 1-215-446-4000. You may discover that you don't have a problem—or that you have a big one.

Averages for expense categories may be particularly telling. You may realize, for example, that your ratio of salary expenses to sales is sky high.

Take a historical view. Talk to people who have held the job before you. Maybe they've dealt with the problem before.

Break the situation into components. Divide and conquer. Look at each aspect of a situation separately. It could be that one element is responsible for the effects you'd like to avoid.

For example, I once had a production-process problem. I isolated each key component—a computer, a computer operator, software, and the information the computer operator started her part of the process with. One by one, I examined each.

The computer operator kept telling me that the problem lay in the software, which blinded me, temporarily, to the real problem: the operator herself. She not only lacked the skill to get the job done but had world-class skills in shifting blame. We got rid of her, and the problems disappeared.

Besides people, equipment and technology, and work processes and practices, don't forget another ever-present element: money and other resources. You may have too little of either—or too much.

Breaking down a problem into components, incidentally, can sometimes help you see that there is a right or a wrong solution to a problem. It helps turn shades of gray into black or white.

Look at the numbers. Good managers watch key measures and ratios in their departments. These may be purely financial, like return on investment, but they may also be productivity measures specific to a particular department. Possibilities include average hours worked on a project, transactions per employee, or sales per employee.

Best Tip

Identify a few key indicators of success for the areas you oversee. If you watch them diligently over time, they'll help you spot problems in the making.

Such measures do no good unless you watch them over time. You get a base-line feel for performance and can spot the roots of a problem. Such measures also serve as "early warning" indicators that help you head off difficulties in the making.

Focus on elements you can control. When defining the

decision to be made, take stock of its elements and focus on those you can control. If you're having trouble selling a product, for example, you can control its price, specifications, and marketing methods, to name a few. You can't control people's reaction to the product directly, and you can't change the overall tastes and preferences of the market. Don't even try.

Expect some "imponderables." Deep problems (especially people problems) usually have imponderable elements. They just don't make sense.

Be aware of imponderables, but don't waste your time. I once had a subordinate who kept shooting himself in the foot by directly disobeying directions, purposely saying the wrong thing at the wrong time, and a host of other ills. I spent way too much time wondering why he did all these things—which delayed me from doing the right thing: removing him from the company.

The Agile Manager's Checklist

✔ Always remember: Superficial solutions are no solution and will set you back farther.

✔ When identifying the roots of a problem,

- Look beyond the "obvious" solution;
- Talk to those closest to the situation;
- Look for cause and effect;
- Ask "Why?" three times;
- Break down the situation into its components;
- Focus on the elements you can control.

✔ Expect some imponderables in any problem—things that don't make sense or that you can't figure out.

Chapter Four

Define the Decision

"So," the Agile Manager said to Wanda, "We have to make a decision. Manuel thinks another analyzer would do it. But the one we have cost $22,000. I'd hate to ask Don for the money for another. He'd turn purple and start foaming at the mouth."

"But I think we need one," Wanda said. "Do you want a riot here?"

"I'm not sure we do need one. It's not just the analyzer. It's the workstation, and the workbench, and an office to have private conversations. Everybody seems discontented. I believe you were right the other day—it's a structural problem. We've added two new people in the past year without considering whether a different structure is appropriate." The Agile Manager brightened. "Let's see if we can solve the problem without buying an analyzer. We don't have much to lose."

Wanda cleared her throat. "I'm not sure I understand. Are you suggesting that we have a workflow problem, and not a space problem? If so, do we need to reevaluate what people do and how they do it?"

"Maybe yes to both questions. It's all still kind of fuzzy in my mind. Whatever we do, we need to get people off each others' backs. Let me tell you about a conversation I had with Anita yester-

day. She wondered whether the group shouldn't work more closely together . . ."

Using the techniques in the last chapter, you should be able to start defining the decision to be made. That means stating what you believe to be the root problem, providing a direction to head in for those who have to come up with solutions, and coming up with concrete objectives for a solution. Identifying a specific goal or two (and usually not more) is the only way you can measure whether a decision solves the problem you are facing.

Start with broad objectives at the highest level possible. Many people start too low. They start defining the parameters of an equipment buy before they've thought through whether they need more equipment. Specifying a broad objective will help you get to that higher level of thinking necessary to making good decisions.

Here are some examples that define a decision to be made and its ultimate objectives.

- "The bottleneck in shipping is a technology problem. We need to revamp the process, most likely using different software and control mechanisms. Whatever we decide, we must eliminate bottlenecks and improve productivity by at least 5 percent."
- "Poor sales on the West Coast are probably due to different tastes. We need to tweak the product slightly and come up with a new marketing angle. Whatever we decide, we must boost sales in the region by 20 percent."
- "People are spending too much time in meetings due to requirements of the team structure. We need to change the structure to avoid so many meetings, and we should consider scrapping the team system altogether. Whatever we decide, we must keep meetings to no more than three hours a week."
- "Heat isn't getting to the northeast part of the building

because of a faulty layout of the duct work. We should probably rearrange the ducts in that part of the building. Whatever we decide, we must make that part of the building habitable."

■ "We're not going to meet our growth goals based on our present product base alone. We need to acquire a product line or company with anywhere from $2 to $5 million in sales. And anything we acquire must be in a business we understand and must promise at least a 22 percent return on the investment."

Best Tip

Define what a decision is supposed to accomplish. It'll guide your actions and provide a benchmark you can use to measure your results against.

■ "Our sales force can't do the job we expect it to. We probably need to add some distributors. Any distributor we decide to use, however, must agree to our terms of a 52 percent discount and payment in thirty days. Also, any arrangement must allow us to cover the South completely and boost sales 15 percent."

■ "We need to revamp our manufacturing process to meet demand and remain competitive. Any new manufacturing method we decide to use must increase throughput by at least 20 percent without adding floor space, or it's not worth doing."

■ "The only way we'll get into this market is through an alliance or an acquisition. Whichever we choose, it should result in a 10 percent market share within three years at the most."

Attaching an objective to the decision is the only way you can evaluate alternative choices. And, once you've made a decision, your objectives will become a yardstick for measuring the decision's success.

Gather More Information

With most problems you spend more than an hour or so pondering, the answer isn't cut or dried. Or there's more than one solution. That's why the problem you've defined should be considered a hypothesis that needs to be tested and bounced off others.

Once you've defined the decision to be made, therefore, you may want to do some more research.

Imagine, for example, that sales are poor on the West Coast because, you believe, tastes there are different and you're marketing the product wrong. That hypothesis has been backed up by anecdotal evidence and a few customer complaints.

But to be certain, you delve deeper. You talk to those who sell the product. You create a survey (unbiased) that goes directly to consumers in the market for a product like yours. You investigate how your competitors are selling their products, and how well they are doing. If it's easy to do, you change an advertisement to deliver a different message. You test its effectiveness.

And you also test your objectives. If you've identified the right problem, you'll want to see increased sales by a certain percentage. Can changing the product and its marketing result in that increase? If not, maybe it's not worth worrying about West Coast sales.

To avoid "analysis paralysis," set a time limit for the information-gathering phase of your work.

As ever, your goal is to find information that backs up or proves your hypothesis. If information refutes your hunch, you formulate another.

Set a Time Limit

You've heard the phrase "analysis paralysis." Managers practice it to avoid making decisions. You can literally spend a lifetime gathering information, so set an artificial time limit: Gather information for a day or a week or a month, then begin to generate alternatives.

Group Decision Making

You can handle small decisions yourself. Big decisions, however, usually demand input from a number of people, including senior managers. If it's appropriate, convene a group to air your view of a problem and what decision may be necessary.

Such meetings are inevitable with important decisions, like what to do about falling sales or whether to get into a new market. (Unless you're a CEO who doesn't care for the input of others. I've known a few of these.)

Big decisions require input from many different people.

Gain a consensus with your fellow decision makers about the nature of the decision before you start generating alternatives. You'll save a lot of time (and a lot of sniping) if you gather informal reactions to your hypothesis. If you don't, expect to be blindsided by hostile people in meetings.

I once read about a job a consultant had done. He'd been hired by a group of the company's senior vice presidents to find an acquisition candidate.

When he completed his research, he met with the vice presidents and the CEO. He made his recommendations, and the CEO started blasting away. "Who says we need to make an acquisition? Who says that's the only way to grow sales? Who says that's the only way to get into that market?" Apparently none of the vice presidents had told the CEO they believed an acquisition was necessary. Seeing his fury, they all remained silent and let the consultant take the full force of his wrath.

Think Ahead

Poor managers are surprised when problems crop up that require immediate attention. When they are always putting out fires, they aren't spending time on real executive work—spotting opportunities, optimizing operations, and hiring well.

Anticipate problems. If you know you're going to need a new piece of equipment or another person in six months, start your research now. When the need becomes pressing, you'll be ready.

The Agile Manager's Checklist

✔ When establishing a framework for a decision, state what you believe to be the real problem and define what the decision is supposed to do.

✔ Even though you have a hunch as to the root cause of a problem, gather more information. You may be surprised.

✔ When making a group decision, be sure everyone first agrees on the nature of the decision to be made and what it should accomplish.

✔ Best advice in the book: Anticipate problems.

Chapter Five

Generate Potential Solutions

"OK everybody, let's get started." The Agile Manager surveyed the ten people around the conference table. They included people from the product-development department as well as one from marketing and another from manufacturing. "It's no secret to all of you that we're getting in each other's way. I'd like to get some ideas on how to solve the problem."

"Buy a new analyzer," yelled Manuel. Everybody laughed.

"I know how you feel, Manuel," said the Agile Manager. "But I want some other ideas. And I want you to forget about money or any other constraint. Let the ideas fly—and no criticizing them. We'll have plenty of time to do that." He ceremoniously walked to the white board set up at the front of the room and wrote, "New analyzer." He turned around and faced the group without saying anything. He held the marker upright, ready to write.

"More floor space," said William.

"Another workstation," said Linda.

"Restructure the work," said Anita. People stopped thinking for a few seconds and looked at her.

"Good," said the Agile Manager.

"Have some of us work at home," said Wanda.

"Outsource design," said Phil. A few people hissed.

41

"No criticizing," said the Agile Manager as he wrote it down.
"Get marketing to format some of our proposals," said Wanda.
"Use simpler designs," said George from manufacturing.
"Stagger hours," said Manuel.
"Work in project teams," said Anita. Again people glanced her
way.
"Have separate offices for all," said William.
"Cut down on the number of products," said Linda. . . .

Now it's time to put flesh to the decision outline you've created by creating a few concrete solutions.

This is the time to be especially flexible and think of alternatives. Every decision profits from competing solutions.

Even when the decision to be made appears clear cut, for
example, you have room for alternatives. Say you're sure you
need another person in your department. Do you? What about
using an outside contractor or reshuffling duties? Or imagine
you're convinced another expensive piece of equipment is the
way to go. What about having vendors bid on the work?

Before You Begin . . .

1. Know your strengths and weaknesses. Use the levers
at your disposal. Your best decisions will arise out of advantages
and strengths. If you find yourself proposing solutions that require you to enter a new business or learn new skills, beware.

A company I'm acquainted with occupies a highly profitable
but specialized and narrow industrial niche. It wanted to grow,
but felt constrained by the niche.

Rather than try to push boundaries outward, or enter a related field, it decided to do something altogether different: Market general business software developed by a consultant that had
done some work for it.

Why? I suspect that to the company software must seem like
a sexy, high-growth field with fewer hurdles and boundaries.
But that's probably because it can't see the hurdles other software companies both see and know well—like the limits of di-

rect marketing, or the sheer number of competitors.

Maybe the company will succeed in its new venture, but I doubt it.

2. Keep resources in mind. When generating alternatives, keep in mind which of the following resources might be the most useful in your situation:

- Money
- Time
- People
- Technology

Know, too, which are available. You may, for example, have to make a decision and implement it quickly, which puts the spotlight on money or technology.

Brainstorm

A tried-and-true method for generating alternatives is brainstorming. Studies show that groups come up with better solutions than if you work alone. Gather the people who are in on the decision, or who will be affected by it, and toss the problem on the table. Let them play with it and come up with creative ways to solve it.

The only guideline should be your conditions, your "must-haves," for the decision. For example, you tell the group, "Whatever we decide, we must reduce expenses 5 percent." That keeps people focused on the decision's ultimate purpose.

Other than that, anything goes. Some guidelines:

Tell people the sky is the limit. Imagine there are no limits or boundaries to a solution.

Forbid critical comments. People should feel free to voice any potential solution.

Stand at a white board or presentation pad. Write down solutions as they come up.

Set a time limit. After a while, ideas degenerate. Thirty to forty-five minutes should be enough time for a session.

Invite people from many disciplines or functions. Participants from different areas improve the quality of the alternatives—everyone present can place a different piece of the puzzle.

Analyze afterwards. Don't stop to think about whether an option might work. Once you have a list, you can sift the junk out and analyze the nuggets you have left. Some may be fool's gold, some real gold.

Create Scenarios

An excellent group decision-making technique is to imagine scenarios that put the decision in perspective.

The U.S. Army, for example, likes to anticipate problem areas in the world they may one day have to police or conduct a war in. Their decisions on how to prepare are helped by the analysis and imagination scenario-building requires.

What do we need to do, the Army might ask, to be ready to fight in Eastern Europe in the middle of winter? Summer? Where would we land if we were called in to defend Taiwan?

When brainstorming, never criticize an idea. You need tons of ideas just to get a few good ones.

Not long before the Gulf War, the Army had wondered how it would deal with a flare-up of tensions in the Middle East, including aggression by certain dictators. It then conducted exercises there that helped enormously when the real conflict came.

Scenarios, then, anticipate and head off high-level problems. Sample questions for businesses include:

- What if Acme's new generator hurts the sales of ours?
- What if Tom should take another job?
- What if Kenzu, Ltd., decides to enter the U.S. market?
- What if the bank refuses to lend us the money?
- What if Placo Corporation sues us for patent infringement?
- What if we offered a stripped down, budget version?

Treasure Counterintuitive Decisions

A good, counterintuitive decision improves your business and befuddles your competitors.

Guy Kawasaki, in *How to Drive Your Competition Crazy*, tells a great story about a mid-scale restaurant in Portland, Oregon, called Old Wives' Tales. The Owner, Holly Hart, needed to increase her business. Instead of thinking linearly and deciding to add seats through expansion, Hart asked a different question: "How can I make dining more pleasant for families?" The answer to this question, she knew, would result in increased business.

When in doubt, choose the option that serves customers, not your operations or your banker.

Hart observed the marketplace and saw families with young children trying to get the meal over with as soon as possible. That gave her an idea. She took out a number of tables and put in an indoor playground. That allowed parents to bring their children out for a meal and relax at the same time. Business boomed.

This story also offers an additional lesson for any in business. Hart's gaze was not on herself, her employees, her banker, or her grounds. It rested upon customers. Serve your customers, and you'll narrow down a range of alternative decisions to those with a real chance of improving your situation.

Eliminate, Substitute, Change

Keep these three words in mind as you generate solutions. Imagine you feel you need to hire another person to get work done in your department. But you'd like to avoid the expense. Your first thought should be, "Can I *eliminate* or reduce some of the work so we don't need to hire?" Perhaps, upon analysis, you're performing work that isn't paying off. Stop doing it, and there goes your problem.

If that doesn't work, ask, "Can I *substitute* a machine or another company to avoid hiring?" An outsourcer might do it better and cheaper. Alternatively, automating part of the process may save you money.

Learn to use and value intuitive techniques for making decisions. Your gut is sometimes as smart as your brain.

If that doesn't work: "Can I *change* how work gets done to avoid hiring?" At a company I once worked for, management decided that the only way to handle a crushing workload for order-entry staff was overtime and more people. The smartest manager, however, refused to accept those as the only choices. He decided to "reengineer" order fulfillment—long before that word became popular—using advanced information technology. The company tripled sales without hiring another person.

Use Intuitive Techniques

Few organizations value intuitive techniques for coming up with solutions to problems as well a means to evaluate decision alternatives. Most of those who oversee decisions want facts and hard analysis to support decisions.

Even the most analytical decision makers, however, should recognize that they usually start with an intuitive idea about a situation and then find facts to support whatever their intuition is telling them.

The best decision makers use both analytical and intuitive techniques to solve problems. Think of Sherlock Holmes. His passion for concrete facts and analysis blind many to his unparalleled capacity to weave together plausible theories using intuition and creativity.

Superagent Mark McCormack, in *What They Don't Teach You at Harvard Business School*, offers another good example of using intuition to aid hard analysis. He advises us to "look around the fringes" of reports or other analytical documents. In other words, if you conduct a marketing study, don't take the results at face value. Try to sense what the report *isn't* telling you explicitly about trends, opportunities, and biases in the marketplace.

That's good thinking, especially when it comes to making decisions about innovative products. Back in the 1950s, IBM predicted a worldwide market for computers numbering in the dozens only. IBM's best minds had no idea what computers could be used for beyond number-crunching. Can you imagine the results of a survey of the general public regarding computers at that time? So much for analysis.

Avoid the problem. Here's a valuable technique to come up with good decisions: Avoid thinking about the problem.

But don't do that until you immerse yourself in it. Fill yourself with details about the decision to be made, then go out and work in the garden. Or on the reproduction Shaker chair in the workshop.

Your subconscious mind continues to work on problems while you attend to other things, then floats thoughts upward when the time is ripe. As you putter around, ideas and solutions come unbidden.

I have my best ideas on long rows, once the endorphins kick in. Correct solutions to problems appear in my mind without warning—and without much effort on my part.

Sitting down and trying to force a decision rarely works. Don't battle yourself. One of you will lose.

Best Tip

Immerse yourself totally in a problem. Then don't think about it for a day. A solution may magically appear.

Try creative writing. Another technique I use profitably is creative writing. Some call it automatic writing, because it seems so effortless.

I'll sit at the computer, for example, and put my decision in question form: "Which strategy should I pursue?" Then I start writing whatever comes into my mind.

Sometimes the results are astonishing. It's as if I'm taking dictation for a wiser, more experienced person than I am. The answer contains insights I hadn't thought of, possible creative courses of action that rise above the narrow channels my mind had been running in, and inspiring encouragement.

The answers are never so simple as "Do this" or "Do that." It's more a process of enlarging my view of a situation, which leads to better decisions.

Where do such thoughts come from? You've heard it said that we use a small part of our brains. Maybe creative writing taps those vast, unused (by the conscious mind) portions of the brain that captures stimuli day in and day out and makes sense of events.

Watch your dreams. Dreams have supplied information that I've used in making decisions to:

- Change jobs;
- Start my own business;
- Distrust (for good reason) people I thought were on my side;
- Trust people I wasn't sure about;
- Establish fresh goals when I've been feeling stale.

Purely rational people, of course, scoff at anyone who would change a job or start a business based on a dream. All I can say is that it works. I wake up, think about what the dream has told me, and alter my course. And in every major decision, the new course has proven fruitful.

It takes time and practice to understand what dreams tell you about your life. Most are laden with symbols that need to be decoded. Fortunately, symbols tend to be personal. You'll see the same ones, or the same scenes, over and over.

For instance, whenever I get bogged down unnecessarily, I have a dream in which I'm standing at a tee on a golf course with a driver in my hand. People are waiting for me to hit the ball, but I can't get comfortable enough to take a swing. I keep adjusting the height of the ball, practicing my swing, checking my grip, and aiming and re-aiming down the fairway.

This dream always spotlights an unconstructive situation, and it helps me refocus and get moving again.

Dream watching, I'm convinced, makes for better decision making. But you have to work at understanding your dreams. That means taking the time to remember them, write them down, and analyze them.

Play "what if." Playing "what if" is like a personal version of brainstorming. You can do it in a group, but you're likely to be less inhibited if you do it alone. That's because you can come up with wacky ideas without fear of anyone laughing at you.

The trick in playing "what if" is to imagine your problem absolutely free of constraints.

Imagine you are trying to figure out a better way to build a house. What if, you ask, I could use any material I wanted? You start listing the possibilities: Paper, iron, mud, grass, glass.

Best Tip

To loosen all boundaries, play "What if?" As in, "What if our products were so affordable that anyone could buy them?"

Innovations rise out of what seem to be ridiculous possibilities. In the western U.S., for instance, straw houses are becoming more popular. Contractors pile hay bales one on top of the other and encase them in stucco walls. The houses are fire resistant and incredibly energy efficient. They stay warm in winter and cool in summer.

Another innovative thinker, playing "what if," imagined a house made of plastic. One result of that thinking is sturdy, rot-proof construction materials (like studs, rafters, and fencing) made out of dense, recycled plastics.

Here where I live in New England, people gather sap in the springtime to make maple syrup. For centuries, they poked a hole in the tree and hung a bucket to collect sap. Then they'd round up the buckets, carry them to the sugar house (as it's called), and boil the sap.

"What if," said an enterprising syrup producer a few decades ago, "I could make the sap come to me instead?" That thought led to plastic tubing arranged so gravity brings the sap directly to the sugar house. "What if," another syrup producer asked not too long ago, "I could make the sap come faster?" That thought led to installing a vacuum pump that pulls sap out the tree faster and increases production significantly.

What ifs are best asked about things you take for granted or things you don't feel you can change. But you always can change them, and therein may lie an advantage for you. "What if we could publish our documentation without using paper?" someone asked. The result: publishing on CD-ROMs and, now, on the World Wide Web.

"Chunk" the problem. Consultant and author Roger Dawson introduced a concept that captures beautifully the manner in which experience improves your ability to make good decisions. It also explains why some people seem to make excellent decisions without giving a matter much thought.

The concept is called "chunking." It's what you do when your intuitive and analytical minds pull together relevant facts and details from your experience rapidly. A decision forms naturally and instantly out of this sea of events and intuitive knowledge.

My wife began having problems very late in her second pregnancy. We went in to have them checked out, and I watched as the doctor felt the position of the baby, poked my wife here and there to see where she was tender, asked her a few questions about how she'd been feeling, and hooked up a monitor to see the baby's heartbeat.

I could see the wheels in his mind turning as all his learning, wisdom, and experience came together to make a quick decision. In all of two or three minutes, he decided to do an emergency Caesarean section. (The baby came out fine.)

Hardly rash, the decision represented twenty years of experience that coalesced in a particular way based on the situation on hand.

How do you chunk? The only way to do it well is to accumulate knowledge and experience—and to be so immersed in your profession or field that you hardly know that you're capable of such feats.

Use Jump Starters

You have to come up with a solution to a problem and you're feeling blue. You can't even begin to come up with an idea, let alone make a decision on it. Do one of two things:

1. Open the dictionary to any page and find a noun or active verb. See how the word sheds light on your situation.

Say you're trying to boost sales of software designed to help people keep track of their finances. You open the dictionary and land on the word "homestead." Ask, "How is my problem like a homestead?"

You notice that one definition of homestead is "a tract of public land granted by the government to encourage development in the West." The government gave away land, remember, to get something in return: productive, taxpaying citizens. Hey, you think, maybe I can give something away. If not early versions of the software itself, what about advice on personal finance?

Best Tip

When you're stuck: Open the dictionary to any page and pick out a word at random. How does it shed light on your situation?

Or coupons that give a discount on books or seminars? You're on your way to solving a problem.

2. Get out the yellow pages. Open it at random and look at the heading at the top right or left of the page. You spot the word "Driveway." How are driveways like my problem? you wonder. Driveways make it easier for people to pull into their garages and park. Is it easy to "pull up to" the software? In every regard? You decide your software is as easy to use as a long, smooth driveway.

What else are driveways good for? They reduce the amount of lawn to be mowed—and hey, they serve as a good basketball court, too. What if I added some kind of game to the software—something that would teach people about taxes or something. I could . . .

Maybe nothing will come of your ideas. But at least you're thinking instead of moping.

Don't Compromise

Sometimes you'll find yourself watering down solutions. "Bob'll never go for it," you say. "Yeah, and besides, the brass will never approve another $14,000 before year end," says someone else. Before long, you're deep into compromise.

Don't compromise before it's time. Most large decisions involve compromise, but that usually happens in the evaluation stage. Come up with the best solutions—backed up with research and analysis and wisdom and experience—before you begin to muddy them up with compromise.

The Agile Manager's Checklist

✔ When generating solutions, keep in mind the levers—your advantages—you can pull.

✔ Brainstorm solutions to sticky problems—and be sure to invite participants from outside your group.

✔ Three concepts to keep in mind as you search for solutions:
- ■ Eliminate
- ■ Substitute
- ■ Change

✔ Work to develop your intuition. It'll save you time and aggravation.

Chapter Six

*E*valuate Alternatives

The Agile Manager had been huddled with Wanda for an hour. She said, in a peevish tone, "Great, we cut the number of products by 10 percent. I don't see how a decision like that solves any problems—and it will probably cut revenue credited to our department. It's just the kind of superficial answer you said we should avoid."

"How so?" he asked.

"I'd be willing to bet you that if we cut back ten percent today, a year from now we'll be back even and climbing. Then everyone will be crawling all over each other again." Wanda stared at him without blinking to let him know how strongly she felt.

"Stop!" he cried, laughing and holding his hands in front of his face. "I hear you." Wanda relaxed.

"OK," he continued. "I can see that maybe I latched on to that idea because I suspect Anita is right. We need to restructure work, probably into teams. And I know how hard it is to get people to change how they work."

"Is that all?" asked Wanda. "I have an antidote for that: Include them every step of the way. That's what I did in my last job. We went from a fairly rigid hierarchy to teams. I gathered everyone *together and playacted. I got quiet and shrugged my shoulders and said, 'People, I'm at a loss. We're supposed to become a team by November. We've all had the training and seen the blueprint, but I don't know how it's going to happen. I need your help.' People felt sorry for me, I think, and we pulled it together."*

"Did it work?" asked the Agile Manager with interest.

"Sort of. It took a year to get the kinks out, but after that things went smoothly. I realized a key was to transfer or get rid of people who didn't fit the system. That was too bad, because I lost a few good people. But they were happier elsewhere and the ones who were left pulled together into a pretty strong unit. We improved productivity 7 percent."

"Hmm. Well, here's what I want to do." Wanda braced herself, knowing the Agile Manager would fire off a laundry list of actions. "Let's look at the impact changing to a team system will have on our operations and those we touch. Maybe there's a reason it won't work. And let's look at that alternative team system Hank was talking about—the one with measures that tracked how well individuals did as well as the team. Also, I want to talk to HR about compensation. And give me a rundown tomorrow on who you think would adapt and who wouldn't. And . . ."

We've come to the most important part of the process, evaluating potential decisions.

It's difficult to evaluate a potential decision well, which is why many decision makers skip this part and go with their instincts only. If you have years of experience in your field, this may be enough. If you don't, you're courting disaster.

Analysis, you'll find, often serves to deflate your optimism or refute your intuition.

That's especially true when you "fall in love" with a house, a job candidate, or an acquisition you simply must have. Simple analysis may show you, for example, that the job candidate who shines in an interview doesn't have the qualifications another candidate has.

This chapter outlines techniques for evaluating decisions. You'll

---

Tool #1: Listen to Your Gut

This is the old standby when evaluating decisions. You know things that haven't reached your conscious mind. Your brain has picked up evidence and signals from a variety of sources and wants you to be aware of its knowledge and conclusions.

Listen to your intuition. It can tell you when to go slow, when to strike, when to doubt a person's word, when you stand face to face with an opportunity, and how to avoid disaster.

The point isn't to listen to your gut and act blindly. Use intuition as a guide. If your intuition is telling you that a person isn't trustworthy, for example, begin to look for evidence that this is true.

Sometimes you don't listen to your intuition. Then you may have a physical reaction. Billionaire investor George Soros, a highly intuitive man, gets a pain in the lower back when he takes a trading position that warrants caution. The pain tells him that something isn't quite right, and he sets about discovering just what the problem is.

The most brilliant business leaders and managers, you'll find, are extremely intuitive. They are the ones who will say, "I make decisions on the spot based on a hunch, and I'm right a majority of the time." They are. Their "touch" may seem magical, but it's based on years of experience, deep thinking about their fields, and learned knowledge. They're chunking (see page 50) full time.

---

also find various evaluating tools sprinkled throughout the chapter. Further, an "interlude" follows that provides examples of financial tools you can use to evaluate decision choices, or to confirm that your decision will pay off.

Encourage Disagreement

Peter Drucker, who should know, reports that Alfred Sloan of General Motors insisted upon disagreement when an important decision needed to be made. He felt it a necessary condition for eliciting the best solution to a problem.

Drucker drew the lesson well and hence minces no words: "The first rule in decision making is that one does not make a decision unless there is disagreement."

Remember that you didn't criticize options when brainstorming? Now consider holding a meeting in which you pick apart solutions to find their flaws. Make sure, however, you observe some ground rules, like:

- Criticize ideas only, not people.

- Criticize constructively. If people can't point out real flaws and propose real solutions, they should remain silent. "I just don't like it" isn't good enough.

- Keep the meeting short—and cut it off altogether if things get nasty.

- Use your best human-relations skills to ensure a positive atmosphere. Remind people that your mutual goal is to get closer to the truth regarding a decision.

- Don't hold meetings like this to decide on the color of the wallpaper in the bathroom. Save them for issues of strategic importance.

Chart Costs and Benefits

By yourself or in a group, perform a simple cost/benefit analysis. Doing so should be enough to knock out a few options. Keep this list in front of you as you work:

Costs: People, disruption to work, distraction from primary duties, misalignment of departments and objectives, material and supplies, equipment, loan interest, reduced profit, R&D, marketing and promotions, legal, time, testing.

Benefits: Increased revenue and profit, market share, return on investment, increased efficiency, prestige or reputation, customer satisfaction, security, quality, good morale, and boosts in the indicators you watch.

Whenever you can, attach numbers to the costs and benefits.

Tool #2: List the Pros and Cons

A time-honored technique for making decisions is to make up a list of pros and cons. It's one of the simplest tools at your disposal, especially when you need to compare one choice to another directly.

Let's say the decision at hand is whether to change jobs.

Pros	**Cons**
More money	Farther commute
Greater authority	Slightly less interesting job
Zippier company	Leave good workmates
International travel	Unknown upward potential
Better Training	No vacation for a year
	Longer workweek
	Work atmosphere unknown

Sometimes, a list like this is enough. You're tired of your current job, and you like the idea of working for a swifter company at a bit more pay. You take the job.

But just as often, you're not sure. So you list the pros and cons of staying where you are.

Pros	**Cons**
Interesting job	Company slow-moving
Good people	Products presently boring
Good upward potential	Money just adequate
Good benefits	Fumbling boss
Close to home	

This list may put things in perspective for you, helping you decide one way or another. If not, try Tool #3.

For instance, "This decision will cost us $35,000 in expenses, overtime, and purchases. It should result in annual savings of $50,000."

This kind of work is better done in groups, especially those with a couple of curmudgeons in it. They'll be sure to deflate your expectations of improved benefits, and they'll think of costs you haven't.

When in doubt, err on the side of fewer or smaller benefits and higher costs. And estimate carefully how long you believe some important action will take. Then double the estimate.

Determine the Impact

Every decision has an impact that reaches farther and wider than you think. Say you decide to go forward with a new product. That decision affects:

- The product-development department
- The company's financial position
- The marketing department
- Order fulfillment
- Warehousing
- Relations with customers
- Competitors (who may retaliate)
- Your company culture
- Relations with distributors.

And others you can probably think of.

Even "small" decisions can have large ramifications. Say you hire someone. You've got to pay her; provide benefits; put her in an office or at a desk with a telephone, computer, and other things; guide her integration into the workflow; and put up with any idiosyncrasies she arrives with.

Or say you buy a single machine that doubles your capacity to produce goods. Are you prepared to double also the rate you sell products, or the size of your warehouse? Big decisions all. And that machine, don't forget, also means:

- Hiring two new people to attend to it;
- Insurance (for years);
- Training costs;
- Maintenance costs (for years);
- A big jump in raw materials to feed it;
- Higher utility bills;
- Interest on a loan, or depleted cash reserves.

Tool #3: Set and Weigh Criteria

After doing a simple list of job-changing pros and cons (Tool #2), you may be more confused than ever. "Wait a minute," you think. "I'm comparing apples to oranges. Is there a way I can compare apples to apples?"

Of course. You establish criteria and weigh each factor based on its importance to you. First list factors important to you, then indicate how important each is by giving it a percentage weight (the total should add up to 100 percent):

Important Factors in My Career
Interesting work—20 percent
Upward potential—20 percent
Job that uses my best skills—15 percent
Good money—15 percent
Good people to work with—10 percent
Supportive bosses—10 percent
Company on the rise—5 percent
Job close to home—5 percent

Now you can set up a matrix as shown and compare the two jobs. Rank the criteria on a scale of 1 to 5, with 5 being the highest, for each job (knowing some rankings will be guesses). Then multiply each score by its weighting factor:

	New Job			Old Job		
	Rank	Weight	Result	Rank	Weight	Result
Interesting work	3	(.20)	.60	4	(.20)	.80
Upward potential	3	(.20)	.60	4	(.20)	.80
Job uses skills	4	(.15)	.60	4	(.15)	.60
Good money	4	(.15)	.60	2	(.15)	.30
Good people	3	(.10)	.30	4	(.10)	.40
Supportive bosses	3	(.10)	.30	2	(.10)	.20
Company on rise	5	(.05)	.25	2	(.05)	.10
Close to home	1	(.05)	.05	5	(.05)	.25
Total			**3.30**			**3.45**

It's close, but your old job is worth sticking with. Now, you think, maybe I can still tell the boss that I've had an offer to see how she reacts . . .

And there's the impact on yourself. How will your daily life change?

Don't Forget Opportunity Cost

When you decide to spend a company resource like money or time, it means you can't spend money or time on something else.

Always ask yourself, "If I choose this option, what will I *not* be able to do in the near future?"

If you spend money on a machine now, what opportunities are you forgoing—due to lack of cash—in the near future? If you decide to devote your resources to pumping up sales of product B, what's going to happen to products A and C?

It's not hard to stop time momentarily and say, "Should we spend to develop a new product or remodel the offices?" It's harder to think out a year or so and anticipate the spending you are giving up to accomplish a goal now. But do the best you can.

Check Your Feelings

Most experts on decision making emphasize coming up with concrete, defensible reasons for deciding to do what you do. (As does this book.)

Yet good decisions aren't always defensible. I recently read of a man who owned a radio station. He'd been offered $13 million for the station, which was nearly seven times what he'd paid for it a few years earlier. He refused the offer, saying, "Selling would be like taking away my soul." While illogical to most, refusing riches and hanging on is the right decision for him.

A company may continue to stay in an unprofitable business because it pays dividends in forms other than money. A company I worked for owned a bookstore that never made money. But it impressed some key contacts in another part of the busi-

Tool #4: Use a Computer Program

A good software program for decision making can automate the process of setting and weighing decision criteria.

Computer programs are most useful when you've decided you want to do something simple, like hire a person or buy a car or house. They help you establish must-have criteria by which to make a good decision, rank and weigh the criteria, and analyze the pros and cons among each choice. Also, they automatically put the weighted criteria in graphic form, like bar graphs. One glance can help you nail down a decision.

A good example is DecideRight by Avantos. (Download a trial version at *www.avantos.com.*)

Though best with apple-to-apple comparisons, you can take such programs a step higher and compare apples to oranges. An example might be a lease/buy decision. Such programs, however, begin to lose their value when you are trying to decide among different options that provide different benefits.

For example, imagine you're deciding whether to keep manufacturing in-house, subcontract it out, or ally yourself with a vendor to get the job done. You can establish a few comparable criteria like price per unit and control over the process. And you can rank and weigh them.

But what about the different benefits and costs that arise out of each situation? For example, if you choose to subcontract out manufacturing, you can chop out part of your payroll expenses. But you also lose good minds working on your behalf. And if you keep manufacturing in-house, you forgo what you'd learn from partnering. As happens with any good decision, you may get confused trying to weigh costs and benefits. The software doesn't help sort things out any better than your brain.

Some computer programs claim to be able to handle complex decisions. Those I've sampled haven't stood up to the challenge. Some are just glorified organizers that allow you to create or attach text files, spreadsheets, databases, and more.

Any program also magnifies human error. What if, through inexperience, you rank price as the most important element in a vendor relationship, when flexibility may be more important?

ness and thus remained untouchable in the eyes of management.

While emotion should play a part in a decision—its the force that lies behind your enthusiasm for a choice—make sure it's tempered by reason. Some people go into a business or introduce a product to "get back at" former employers or "teach a lesson" to upstart competitors. Often they end up regretting the decision.

Ask Six Questions

When evaluating solutions, six questions will help you see whether you can put alternatives into practice. Rudyard Kipling called them his "six serving men," to be used in all kinds of situations:

- Who?
- What?
- Where?
- Why?
- When?
- How?

Posing any one of these questions could highlight flaws in a proposed decision. For instance, you may have a great solution but not the right person to implement it. You decide on an alternative.

You need good answers to each of these questions before you move forward.

Get Expert Opinion

When publishing companies are unsure whether to publish a manuscript, they send it around to a number of experts in the field for an opinion. They aren't looking for everyone to say, "This is great!" They just want to know it's publishable and has a fair chance of success. And they want to know about major flaws in thinking or execution.

Likewise, companies often hire consultants to assess the alternatives. Be careful how you use consultants, though. Poor managers often use them to avoid making decisions themselves.

Plan to Measure Outcomes

One way to evaluate alternatives is to ask, "Can we measure the outcome of the decision?" You must have early feedback on your choice if you want an opportunity to cut your losses.

A smart businesswoman I know had a successful bookstore. She opened another one in a seemingly choice location. She closed it in less than six weeks. Sales were so far from her projections that there was no doubt in her mind the location was a loser.

You should be able to measure your decision against the goals you set for it—the must-haves the decision is supposed to yield.

Easy measures are sales, profitability, staying on time and within budget, and improving productivity.

Resist soft measures. For example, say one of your options for restructuring is to move to a team system. How will you know if it's working? Anecdotal evidence isn't good enough—"Oh yeah, everyone is happier and we seem to be getting a lot more work done." Decide in advance that you'll chart progress based on speedier processes, improved productivity, fewer people get-

---

Tool #5: Flip a Coin

When you're unsure what to do, flipping a coin is a great way to make yes/no and go/no go decisions, and decisions between two options. Don't laugh yet—this method offers a twist you'll find useful.

Say something like "Heads I decide to go with choice A, and tails I go with choice B."

Flip the coin and note the answer. Here's the twist: How do you feel about the choice that comes up—good or bad? That's your intuition talking. It may be telling you something worth listening to.

ting more work done, reduced costs, or whatever makes sense for your situation.

Imagine the Best and Worst Cases

Imagine, in specific detail, how an alternative would fare under both the best circumstances and the worst.

Because you'll naturally fall into thinking optimistically, spend more time forming worst-case scenarios. If the worst isn't so bad, you don't have much to lose. If the worst case will sink the company, reject it outright.

Imagine the total range of possibilities. What happens if an alternative performs neither brilliantly nor poorly? Is it worth pursuing an option that's, say, just above break-even?

When evaluating an alternative, imagine in detail the worst outcome. Can you live with it? If not, back to work.

Especially beware if chances are against something working unless the exact right conditions contrive to produce a miracle. Go for the miracle—maybe—when your back is against the wall, but at no other time.

Consider the worst, too, when buying a machine. You may blind yourself to the risk by saying something like, "Well, we can always sell it for $10,000 or so." Are you sure?

Just before the desktop publishing revolution, I bought a used typesetting machine I felt would "always" be worth at least $2,000 or so. Ha. Its value fell to zero overnight.

Be careful too, with inventory. I've had warehouses filled with merchandise that I couldn't give away. In the end I paid to have it hauled to the dump. Residual value? Negative in this case.

Avoid Temporary Solutions

In the town where I grew up, the government built temporary housing for veterans returning home from World War II. That "temporary" housing—Quonset huts—remained on the

Tool #6: Evaluate with the Data at Hand

If you're in business, you most likely have a mountain of data to help you make decisions.

These will probably be most useful when compared to other figures—historical figures from your own company, industry averages, or "ideal" figures you come up with.

For instance, say you're deciding whether to hire another person or automate part of a process, eliminating the need for the new hire. You do a little figuring and realize that sales per employee are $293,500. Hey, pretty good, you think. But then you go to the library and consult data from Robert Morris Associates, and you discover that the average company in your industry and at your revenue level has sales per employee of $356,400. You opt for automating the process.

Another example: You're trying to figure out whether to restructure your company. You have a vague feeling that productivity is down, so you study the situation.

You discover that all through the 1980s and early 1990s, productivity, based on transactions per employee, increased by about 3 percent a year. For the past few years, however, the figure has been flat. And last year it actually fell by a point.

That confirms it, you think. Whatever we're doing, it's not working. We need to restructure to get productivity climbing again.

Hard data you can use to make decisions include:

- Sales or profitability figures
- Productivity
- On-time delivery
- Cycle time
- Number of employees
- Machine breakdowns
- Employee costs
- Cost of goods sold
- Throughput time
- Expenses in any category
- Taxes
- Earnings per share

banks of the canal for fifteen years, an eyesore and of little value to anyone. (Who'd want to live in a Quonset hut for more than six months?) Yet the price was always right for someone.

All of this is to say that temporary solutions turn permanent.

Best Tip

Temporary "solutions" often turn into long-term problems that refuse to go away.

As I write, the U.S. House of Representatives is considering temporary spending programs to avoid inflating the budget deficit. How often are spending programs cut back in the U.S.? (Or anywhere else, for that matter?)

Temporary solutions mask a refusal to deal with underlying problems. And they'll haunt you longer than you want.

Reduce the Risk

Often when you evaluate alternatives, one will seem enticing. But you may feel the risk is higher than you'd like to take on. Here are a few options to reduce risk:

Seek alternative financing. Lease rather than buy. Or take a loan out rather than use your own cash.

Scale back the decision. Maybe you can introduce a version of a product without all the features you'd originally envisioned, or introduce it in a single region.

Gather more information. Maybe you need to do one more market survey. Japanese electronics companies are famous for creating products designed solely for sale in Tokyo's Ginza district. If a product flies there, they roll it out nationally.

Find a partner with money or knowledge you don't have.

Plan a number of "bail out" points along the way. A company I worked for started a new publication. We identified the number of subscribers we wanted by each issue for the first three years. I'm happy to report that the company was brave and disciplined enough to bail out after the very first issue and cease operations.

Tool #7: Ask for a Symbol

Here's an intuitive technique for those of you who liked the techniques employing dreams and creative writing: Ask yourself for a symbol—a mental image—that contains an answer to a problem.

This method works. You're tapping parts of the brain that hum along day after day just beneath your conscious awareness. The symbol the mind produces is a concentrated answer that you need to ponder or decode.

I'll never forget going house hunting and visiting a house occupied by an elderly couple who couldn't afford to keep it in good shape. The price was right, and we started to think seriously about making an offer. I asked myself for a symbol.

In a rush, and in frightening detail, my subconscious created an image in which the furnace in the house turned into a multi-armed monster that consumed the house. Wow, I said. I wonder what that means.

It wasn't hard to figure out. The heating plant in the house was very old and inefficient. It burned far more oil to produce heat than would a modern system. In addition, the house was poorly insulated and lacked a lot of the insulating features we take for granted in the Northeast, like door sweeps, weather-stripping, and insulated curtains.

My brain absorbed all of this information—even things I hadn't noticed—and sent me a message, via the symbol, loud and clear: "You buy this house, and it will consume you."

Give this technique a try right now. Think of a situation that is nagging you, like a problem you can't solve, a decision you can't make, or a situation you can't understand. Ask for a symbol. If you don't impede it, one will pop into your mind.

It's a gift, so treat it as such.

Change the timing. Launch a product in the fall rather than in the spring, for instance. Start an effort later than you wanted but after everyone has had some training.

Keep in mind how rewards change as you reduce the risk. For

example, if you call in a partner on a project, you have to share the benefits. It may be well worth sharing benefits—or you may conclude it's a waste of time.

Do Nothing

At this point in your deliberations, it's good to remember you still have a potent choice: Do nothing.

If you choose to do nothing, make it a deliberate choice for good reasons. (And here, a good reason may be your intuition screaming, "Don't do it!") Don't let opportunities wither from

---

Tool #8: Rank Using the 'Tic Tac Toe' Method

This is a good method to use when you have many options. Say, for example, you want to develop two products. Your developers and marketers come up with eight competing options. What do you do? Rank each one against all the others. Take an option and go across the list, pitting it against each other option. Whenever it "wins," give it one point. When it loses, zero.

Here is an example:

	A	B	C	D	E	F	G	H		TOTALS
A	X	1	1	0	0	1	1	1	=	5
B	0	X	0	0	0	1	0	0	=	1
C	0	1	X	1	1	0	0	1	=	4
D	1	1	0	X	0	1	1	0	=	4
E	1	1	0	1	X	0	1	1	=	5
F	0	0	1	0	1	X	1	1	=	4
G	0	1	1	0	0	0	X	1	=	3
H	0	1	0	1	0	0	0	X	=	2

When you're done, tally up the score for each option by adding up each row. In our case, products A and E come out ahead. They're the ones we'll develop.

neglect. Poor managers delay decisions until the opportunity becomes stale and unpalatable under any circumstances. They say, happily, "Oh well, too late to do anything about that."

The Agile Manager's Checklist

✔ Balance your intuition with sound analysis.

✔ Find people who disagree with your potential decision and understand their reasons.

✔ For major decisions, always create a chart of costs and benefits.

✔ Think through the impact the decision will have on others.

✔ Employ Kipling's Six Serving Men: Who, what, where, why, when, and how.

✔ Figure out a way to measure the outcome of your decision, then watch that measure carefully.

Financial Tools for Evaluating Alternatives

Few decisions can't be put to a financial test. You can, for example, estimate the cost of a bad hire, or you can identify the revenue potential of a number of alternative strategies.

Wise managers quantify their decisions. They know it's often the only way to get projects and proposals past senior managers, who guard the money. The big question in the minds of executives will be, always, "How will this decision affect sales and profits?"

Never say you want to do something, for example, "because it's a good idea," or because "morale would go up." Do something because you'll get a "22 percent return on the investment," or because "costs in shipping will go down at least 14 percent." And have the figures and analysis to prove the value in whatever you propose.

In certain situations, using financial tools isn't merely helpful, it's absolutely necessary. When you buy production equipment, for example, you need to do a payback analysis. When you acquire another company, you need to project exactly what the acquisition will cost in today's dollars, as well as give an honest projection of the investment's potential return.

Let's run through a few examples of financial tools at your disposal, going from the simplest to the more complex (but ultimately more useful).

Note #1: All the financial tools you'll read about here generate hard numbers. The results may lead you to believe you have a sure thing. *Never, ever* forget, however, that the results these tools help you project are based, for the most part, on estimates. You guess how many units you can sell, for example, or what your profit margin will be. That's why it pays to do extensive research to come up with figures, and to be as conservative as you can. When in doubt, jack up expenses and reduce sales or units sold.

Note #2: Some of these tools, like net present value, are more easily computed using a spreadsheet program for computers. Or you can use the little financial calculators Hewlett-Packard makes. You can also write out the details of your decision options and bring them down to Stan in the finance department. He may love to help you out. Or bring them home to Miriam, your sister-in-law the accountant.

Return on Investment

Return on investment (ROI) is simple to figure, but of only limited use. Here's the formula:

$$\text{ROI} = \text{Net Income/Investment}$$

Say you invest $100,000 to enter a new business, and you earn $16,000 a year after expenses. ROI is 16 percent.

You could also substitute new cash flow for net income in the formula, as this example shows: You buy a piece of production equipment that costs $10,000. It will save you $3,000 a year that you now pay a vendor. Your ROI is 30 percent.

Sounds good, but in neither case have we identified how long the investment will return at those rates. What if the machine breaks down after two years? You're in the hole. And don't forget that the machine will increase some expenses, lowering the return.

Payback Analysis

Payback analysis is a straightforward tool that takes time and expenses into consideration. It helps you figure out when your investment—in a machine or a person, for example—pays for itself and begins to earn money.

Here's the formula:

Investment/Net Income (per year) = Payback Period

Let's say you buy a machine that will help you pump out more goods. It costs $20,000 and will produce 2,500 units a year. Each unit sells for $10. After subtracting selling expenses and cost of goods sold and overhead, you clear $2 per unit or $5,000 total.

$20,000/$5,000 = 4 years.

Is the payback fast enough? That's up to you to decide.

You could also do a payback analysis by estimating the cost savings a machine will yield. Maybe you'd like to spend $24,000 to replace an aging machine. It's faster than the old one, and it won't require as much money to maintain. You figure it'll save you $3,500 per year.

$24,000/$3,500 = 6.86 years.

That's a fairly long payback period for a machine, so you decide to refurbish your present one and stick with it.

Break-even Analysis

Break-even analysis is similar to payback analysis, but it can be used for more complex situations—like expanding, acquiring a business, or introducing a product.

Your goal is to figure out what level of sales or units sold will cover your fixed costs (like overhead) and the variable expenses you have for each unit sold. Variable costs are those that rise and fall with your level of sales or production—materials, direct labor, certain plant costs, or selling expenses, for example.

Here's an example in which we calculate break-even according to the number of units sold, a variation on figuring break-even sales. The formula:

Break-even Volume in Units = Fixed Costs/Marginal Profit

Say you'd like to introduce a new product. You've run all the numbers and you believe you can sell, over time, 100,000 units of the product at $15 each. Here's a breakdown of sales, costs and income:

	Total	**Per Unit**
Sales:	$1,500,000	$15.00
Expenses:		
Fixed	224,000	2.24
Variable	1,089,000	10.89
Income	187,000	1.87

The first thing to figure is marginal profit. That's revenue minus variable expenses. In this case, it's $15–10.89, or $4.11 per unit. That's how much money you have, per unit, to cover your fixed costs. Dividing $224,000, your fixed costs, by $4.11 shows you'll have to sell 54,501 units to break even.

Your main question at this point: Can you sell that many units at that price in an acceptable amount of time?

It would probably be useful to vary the selling price to see how different price points compare.

CONTRIBUTION MARGIN. You can also look at break-even in terms of "contribution margin." That's marginal profitability expressed as a percentage. The formula:

Contribution Margin = (Price – Variable Costs)/Price.

In the case above, contribution margin equals (15–10.89)/15, or 4.11/15. That's 27.4 percent.

Now you can use that figure to come up with, among other things, a break-even level of sales.

Break-even Sales = Fixed Costs/Contribution Margin.

In our case, that's $224,000/.274, or $817,518. Of course, you could have multiplied 54,501 by $15 to get the same answer.

WHAT IF WE NEED TO MAKE A PROFIT? Break-even analysis shows you how many units or how much sales you need to get to the point of zero profit. What if you figure you need to make, say, a 10 percent profit?

Simple. Include that figure as a variable cost. Using the same example, we could add $1.50 (10 percent of $15) to our variable costs of $10.89. The result is $12.39. Plugging the new figure into the formula for contribution margin, we get: (15–12.39)/15, or 2.61/15 or 17.4 percent.

(An easier way: Subtract 10 percent from our original contribution margin of 27.4 percent.)

Thus, 224,000/.174= $1,287,356. That's break-even sales that includes a 10 percent profit. Dividing it by $15 gives us the number of units we must sell: 85,824.

That puts things in more useful perspective, huh?

COMPANYWIDE BREAK-EVEN. It's sometimes useful to look at break-even at a companywide level.

The formula:

Break-even Sales = Fixed Expenses + Variable Expenses (Expressed as a Percentage of Sales)

For example, say you sell a range of products and, and your variable costs average 56 percent of sales. Fixed expenses, like overhead and loan payments, come to $1.1 million. Plugging the figures into our formula:

Break-even sales = $1.1 + .56 (sales) [or x=1.1+.56x]

Isolating sales (x) using simple algebra, we get break-even sales of $1.1 divided by .44, or $2.5. Anything over $2.5 million is profit (minus variable expenses associated with new sales).

Analysis of this sort could be useful if you're thinking about expanding. You estimate new fixed expenses and potential new revenue, and plug in your present ratio of variable expenses to sales.

CAVEAT: Payback and break-even analysis are useful tools to help you make decisions. But neither one takes into account the time value of money. To do that, you need more powerful tools.

Time Value of Money

When you're making an important decision on where and how to invest capital, you need to show the effects time has on money.

Why is this important? Let's take a simple example. Say your brother-in-law weasels out of you a snowmobile you're not using. He says, "I'll pay you $6,000 for this in five years. My kids will be out of the house then, and I'll have more money." You figure the machine is worth about $6,000, and you've had a few beers, so you go along with the idea.

The next morning you have misgivings. And for good reason. You weren't thinking about how inflation erodes money. Nor were you thinking about the value of having $6,000 in hand now, so you could invest it and earn interest.

Upon thought, you figure your money should be getting a 10 percent return. That covers the effects of inflation and a little interest to get you through cold nights.

This table shows what today's $6,000 is worth based on a 10 percent rate of interest every year for the next five years. The figure under Year 5 is future value of the $6,000 —and what your brother-in-law *should* pay you when the debt comes due.

Present	Year 1	Year 2	Year 3	Year 4	Year 5
$6,000	$6,600	$7,260	$7,986	$8,785	$9,663

As the following table shows, however, you get (in effect) $3,726, which is what your $6,000 will be worth in five years in today's dollars (discounted 10 percent for inflation and the interest you are foregoing).

Present	Year 1	Year 2	Year 3	Year 4	Year 5
$6,000	$5,455	$4,958	$4,508	$4,098	$3,725

If he's a nice guy, he'll renegotiate. But don't count on it.

Let's see how we arrived at those figures. We need to consult a couple of tables. The first, at the top of the next page, shows what today's dollars are worth, at various rates, in the future

Future Value of $1 at Various Rates

Years	1%	2%	3%	4%	5%	6%	7%	8%	9%	10%
1	1.0100	1.0200	1.0300	1.0400	1.0500	1.0600	1.0700	1.0800	1.0900	1.1000
2	1.0201	1.0404	1.0609	1.0816	1.1025	1.1236	1.1449	1.1664	1.1881	1.2100
3	1.0303	1.0612	1.0927	1.1249	1.1576	1.1910	1.2250	1.2597	1.2950	1.3310
4	1.0406	1.0824	1.1255	1.1699	1.2155	1.2625	1.3108	1.3605	1.4116	1.4641
5	1.0510	1.1041	1.1593	1.2167	1.2763	1.3382	1.4026	1.4693	1.5386	1.6105
6	1.0615	1.1262	1.1941	1.2653	1.3401	1.4185	1.5007	1.5869	1.6771	1.7716
7	1.0721	1.1487	1.2299	1.3159	1.4071	1.5036	1.6058	1.7138	1.8280	1.9487
8	1.0829	1.1717	1.2668	1.3686	1.4775	1.5938	1.7182	1.8509	1.9926	2.1436
9	1.0937	1.1951	1.3048	1.4233	1.5513	1.6895	1.8385	1.9990	2.1719	2.3579
10	1.1046	1.2190	1.3439	1.4802	1.6289	1.7908	1.9672	2.1589	2.3674	2.5937

All you do is look at the figure for 10 percent (top row) and follow it down for five years. You get 1.6105. That's what today's $1 is worth in five years at a 10 percent annual interest rate. Multiply $6,000 by 1.6105 and you get—voilà—$9,663.

The table at the top of the next page shows what today's money is worth discounted at various rates. (In other words, the rate at which inflation and interest forgone erode your money.)

Look again at the column labeled 10 percent, go down to year five, and you find .6209. That's what your dollar today is worth five years from now. Multiply .6209 by $6,000 and you get $3,725.40. And that's how your crafty brother-in-law got a great deal on the snowmobile.

Let's look at another example, using the future value table.

Say someone wants to buy your business for $750,000. She'll pay you over ten years. You like that price, but you want to make ⸱re you get all of that $750,000 in today's dollars. You look in ɪr crystal ball and decide inflation will run about 3 percent a

Present Value of $1 at Various Rates									
Years	**1%**	**2%**	**3%**	**4%**	**5%**	**6%**	**7%**	**8%**	**9%**	**10%**
1	.9901	.9804	.9709	.9615	.9524	.9434	.9346	.9259	.9174	.9091
2	.9803	.9612	.9426	.9246	.9070	.8900	.8734	.8573	.8417	.8264
3	.9706	.9423	.9151	.8890	.8638	.8396	.8163	.7938	.7722	.7513
4	.9610	.9238	.8885	.8548	.8227	.7921	.7629	.7350	.7084	.6830
5	.9515	.9057	.8626	.8219	.7835	.7473	.7130	.6806	.6499	.6209
6	.9420	.8880	.8375	.7903	.7462	.7050	.6663	.6302	.5963	.5645
7	.9327	.8706	.8131	.7599	.7107	.6651	.6227	.5835	.5470	.5132
8	.9235	.8535	.7894	.7307	.6768	.6274	.5820	.5403	.5019	.4665
9	.9143	.8368	.7664	.7026	.6446	.5919	.5439	.5002	.4604	.4241
10	.9053	.8203	.7441	.6756	.6139	.5584	.5083	.4632	.4224	.3855

year for the next ten years.

As the table shows, at an interest rate of 3 percent a year, a dollar today is worth $1.3439 in ten years. Multiply $750,000 by 1.3439 and you get $1,007,925. Divide that figure by ten, and you get your yearly payment for ten years: $100,792.50.

Tables like these help you see the real ravages of inflation—a measly 3 percent rate means you need an extra $250,000 over ten years just to stay even!

Present Value in Action

Present value calculations are a great way to decide among competing investment alternatives, as the following example shows.

First, understand that present value calculations require a "discount factor." Also known as the hurdle rate, it's discussed in detail below. Right now, be aware that it represents the return management wants on its money (or the full cost of borrowing)

Here's an example. Say you need to buy a new piece of pr duction equipment and, after study, realize you face three g options:

1. Buy Machine A. It costs $20,000 and will last three years. It costs $2,000 a year to operate and maintain.

2. Buy Machine B. It costs $15,000 and will also last three years. It has the same capacity as Machine A, but it costs $4,000 a year to operate.

3. Lease a Machine. It has the same capacity as the others. Cost: $9,950 a year.

Because the machines produce exactly the same type and number of products, the only way to choose among them is to analyze costs connected to them. And the only way to determine those costs accurately is to determine what the present value of future costs will be.

Our discount factor, you'll note, is a low 6 percent.

Machine	Initial Cost	Cost Year 1	Cost Year 2	Cost Year 3	Present Value at 6%
A	$20,000	$2,000	$2,000	$2,000	$25,346.02
B	$15,000	$4,000	$4,000	$4,000	$25,692.05
Lease	0	$9,950	$9,950	$9,950	$26,596.47

All the options are pretty close, but it looks like Machine A wins here. Its costs have a present value of $25,346.02 at 6 percent, which represents total costs in today's dollars.

How did we arrive at the figures for total costs? The math involved is beyond the scope of this book. But you can do just what we did—plug the figures into a spreadsheet program like Excel or Quattro Pro and let it figure out the answer. You'll face a bit of a learning curve in determining how to set up the problem, but it's well within the grasp of everyone reading this book—even numberphobes.

Net Present Value

Net present value is the present value minus the money invested over the life of the project.

In this example, we'll analyze whether it's worth buying another production machine given the amount of money it'll cost to purchase and maintain. We'll use the same hurdle rate of 6 percent. (That's pretty low—we're not doing much more than covering the effects of inflation.)

Whereas before we looked only at costs, here we're looking at both costs and sales. We want to make sure the present value of costs and sales combine to create a positive cash flow.

	Initial Cost	Year One	Year Two	Year Three	PV @ 6%	PV Annualized Cost	PV Annualized Sales
Added Expense							
New Machine	$20,000	2,000	2,000	2,000	25,346	(8,448)	
New Overhead	10,000	1,000	1,000	1,000	12,673	(4,224)	
Added Income							
Increased Sales		12,000	15,000	18,000	42,171		14,057
				Total present value costs		(12,672)	
				Annual net present value			**$1,385**

As you can see, the machine provides an annual positive cash flow of $1,385. That figure is good enough to convince us to buy the machine, because we have a 6 percent rate built into the figures. (Anything over $0 would be good enough.)

Cost of Capital and Hurdle Rate

How do you come up with the discount factor essential to computing net present value? That depends in part on your cost of capital, which depends on the marginal cost of capital—what your *next* dollar of capital costs you to borrow, and not the (probably) lower average cost.

What if you don't need to borrow money to invest? Then you should be concerned with the *opportunity* cost of capital—what opportunities you are forgoing to invest in a project. For example, would you invest in a product that will earn 5 perce when you can invest in the stock market and make 10 perce

The clearest definition of cost of capital I have found comes from a book long out of print, *ROI: Planning for Profitable Growth* by Richard Stockton. He says, "A firm's cost of capital represents the average return on investment that its investors expect to earn over time."

Cost of capital is an integral part of the "hurdle" rate senior managers set. That's the minimum rate of return they want on any investment. For some companies, the hurdle rate is the marginal cost of capital. For others, it's cost of capital plus other factors, like the historic rates of return the company is used to getting on new projects, the value of competing opportunities within (or outside) a business, and more. In other words, in some companies the hurdle rate has more to do with what's going on inside the business than outside (the cost of borrowing).

That's why the hurdle rate at some companies might be as low as 15 percent and, at others, as high as 35 percent. (And the hurdle rates may vary within companies depending on the investment's risk factor.)

Don't try to figure out the hurdle rate—just ask a senior manager what it is for new investments. The rate of return for a project should beat that rate. If it does, and your analysis and case for a new investment are sound, you should get approval.

Flow Chart the Decision

A flow chart shows the possible outcomes of a group of related decisions and their financial impact. Charting the decision is valuable because it illustrates graphically the probable results of decisions you make. This is especially helpful when one big decision is made up of many others.

Here's a simple example. Suppose you have an idea for a product. You estimate the likelihood of its success at 50 percent, but it'll cost $50,000 to do a test to show if you'll be successful. Should you do it? Before we answer that, let's get some details.

If the test shows the product is marketable, you estimate the product will bring in $125,000 in after-tax cash flow each

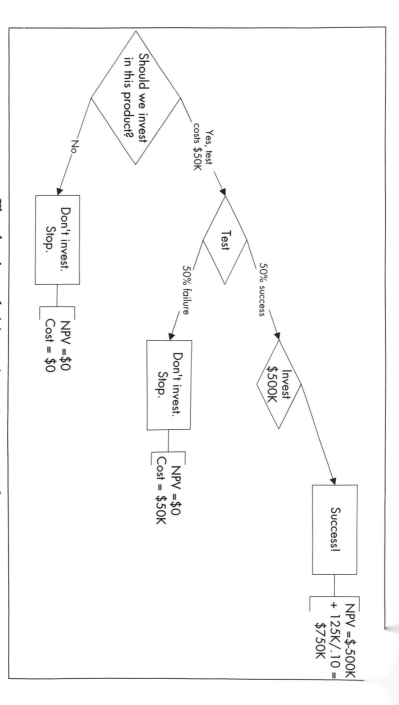

Flowcharting a decision to invest in a new product.

year in perpetuity. But first you'll have to spend $500,000 to remodel the plant and buy new equipment.

And since we're dealing with a large sum of money in the future, we have to take into consideration the time value of money. In this case, we set the discount rate at 10 percent. That covers the effects of inflation and opportunities forgone.

A calculation shows the net present value of the new product, if successful, at $750,000.

What is the real decision to be made? That's easier to see when you put the sequence into graphic form as we did on the previous page.

As the chart shows, first you have to decide whether to test or not. If you decide to test, you have a 50 percent chance of failure. In that case, you're out $50,000 and presumably wiser. But if you succeed, you need to decide whether to invest the $500,000 or not. If you can scrounge up the money, it's a good bet, because the net present value exceeds the initial investment by $750,000.

Seeing the information graphically helps put the decision in perspective by clarifying the costs and payoffs. It especially helps by highlighting the big decision: whether to spend the $50,000 to see if we can make $750,000.

The key to coming up with an honest appraisal of an opportunity lies in forecasting probabilities accurately. Forecasting is most reliable when it is based upon sound estimates, and when you've taken the time to understand the details by visualizing them (as in a flow chart) and by analyzing them using math.

Price Your Products

Another common decision is how to price the products or services you sell.

Before we outline a couple of methods, keep in mind the pricing method used by most successful manufacturers. Start with a price you believe will result in acceptable sales, then figure out how to produce the item profitably.

I've worked places where decision makers figured the cost of producing an item, tacked on an arbitrary figure for profit, and called it a price. Sometimes it worked, sometimes not.

With that in mind, here are two methods to price a product:

1. Turn profit into a "fixed" cost. Start with a variation on the contribution margin formula:

**Contribution Margin =
Fixed Costs (including profit)/Volume (in units)**

For this method to work, you need to be fairly certain how many units you can sell, and you have to identify the total profit you'd like to have.

Using the numbers from the example on page 73, and setting our profit figure at $110,000, we get:

Contribution Margin = $224,000+110,000/100,000 units.

This yields a contribution margin of $3.34 per unit. Add that figure to the variable costs per unit, or $10.89, to yield a potential price of $14.23. Will the market bear this price? Your call.

2. Set up a pricing table. Pricing tables look official and authoritative, but they are the result of someone's educated guess about how changes in price would affect volume.

Here's an example. Let's say that fixed costs remain constant at $75,000, and you have $4.25 in variable costs per unit. Note that total profit will at some prices be greater with reduced vol-

Retail Price	Volume	Revenue	Fixed Costs	Variable Costs	Total Costs	Total Profit
$14	13,000	$182,000	75,000	55,250	130,250	51,750
$15	12,000	180,000	75,000	51,000	126,000	54,000
$16	10,500	168,000	75,000	44,625	119,625	48,375
$17	9,500	161,500	75,000	40,375	115,375	46,125
$18	9,000	162,000	75,000	38,250	113,250	48,750
$19	8,600	163,400	75,000	36,550	111,550	51,85(
$20	7,500	150,000	75,000	31,875	106,875	43,1

ume. You may have reasons for foregoing greater profit, such as when you want to increase market share. But in general, find the point of highest profit and price accordingly.

You can produce a pricing table for one of your own products without much trouble—except for coming up with the numbers in the second column!

Watch the Numbers

The great thing about making decisions based on the analyses presented here is that you have measures to gauge your success. Are you achieving the cash flows you'd hoped for? Why not? What can you do about the situation?

Average managers use numbers to make decisions. Superior managers use numbers to make decisions and follow up on them.

The Agile Manager's Checklist

✔ Quantify your decisions as best you can. Your organization's senior managers will be looking for the benefits of any proposal put in terms of dollars.

✔ Get to know these formulas:

- ROI = Net Income/Investment
- Payback Period = Investment/Net Income (per year)
- Contribution Margin = (Price − Variable Costs)/Price

✔ Always take into consideration the time value of money. Inflation erodes it at a horrendous pace (even when inflation is low).

✔ Know your company's "hurdle rate."

Chapter Seven

Decide and Implement

"No, it's a project team system," said the Agile Manager in response to a question. He'd gathered people in the department together to announce the decision he'd made. "Each three-person team will be responsible for a project from start to finish. That doesn't mean you can't engage others now and then. But the team will have responsibility and accountability."

"You mean," said William, "That I won't be doing the computer design for every product?"

"Right." The Agile Manager looked at William, who seemed to want to say something. When he didn't, he continued. "You see, Wanda and I—and many of you—believe there's some overlap the way things are set up now. That's why you're getting in the way of each other. And that's why you, Will, are swamped with work. Everybody's asking you to get the design into the computer. And when you're swamped, things slow down and people shift to things they can accomplish. Then we get bottlenecks elsewhere, like at the analyzer."

"But who else will do computer design?" asked William.

"You'll train someone," said the Agile Manager. "And you'll be trained to do other things besides design. You'll learn new skills."

"I'm assuming," said Manuel, "That if it doesn't work we'll go back to the way we do things and maybe just buy more equipment. Right?" He spoke with the tone of someone who didn't expect to be contradicted.

"Wrong," said the Agile Manager. At least I hope you're wrong, he thought. "There's no going back. This change will take a while to get used to, a year or maybe even more. But we believe that in the long run we'll work more efficiently with the resources we now have."

"Who am I working with?" asked Anita.

"We'll cover that tomorrow."

"Um," said Phil, staring at the table. "I've never really been good working with people. I mean, I don't have a hard time. It's just that I like to set my own schedule. You know what I mean?"

"Yes," said the Agile Manager. "First let me say that HR is setting up a training program in team skills that will start on Friday. It'll be an hour every other day for two weeks. But also, Phil, it may be that you can continue to work the way you like. You'll have to work it out with your teammates—and adapt yourself slightly to their rhythm, most likely." Phil didn't look happy.

"Some of you may not like the system," said Wanda. "It takes getting used to. Done well, it pays off. You'll work faster without more effort, for one thing. For another, you'll all share in some new bonus money based on results. But I have to say that I'd guess at least a few of you won't adapt to the system." Like you, Phil, she thought.

"Then what?" asked William with a look of genuine fear.

"I'm sure we'll both figure it out," said Wanda with a convincing smile. "You'll have options."

"What's this about a bonus?" asked Manuel.

"Here's how it works . . ."

No doubt you hoped that one decision alternative leapt out at you and said, "I'm the one!"

It rarely happens. In my hiring upwards of a dozen employees, for example, only once was a candidate head-and-shoulders above the others. And even he didn't have all the must-haves I was looking for.

Complicated problems—like how to boost revenue, which product to develop first, where to cut costs, which vendor to partner with—rarely yield simple solutions. That's why it's important not to get swamped by detail or wait for the perfect solution to come along.

And in the long run, it may not matter which decision you make. Mark McCormack, writing in *What They Don't Teach You at Harvard Business School*, says decisions are self-fulfilling. What he means is that once you make a choice,

> ## *Best Tip*
>
> If you really hustle, you can often make a bad decision turn out OK.

you can hustle to make it work. Even a bad decision. That explains why entrepreneurs new to a field start companies that no one with experience in it would start—and succeed.

McCormack's theory has a downside, too: You can undermine a good decision if you start second-guessing yourself. You won't give it the respect it deserves, and your misgivings will turn into a lack of confidence and, ultimately, failure.

All this should make it easier—at least slightly—to make a decision.

Bet the Company?

In their excellent book *Built to Last*, Jerry Porras and James Collins describe the traits that make companies great. Given a choice, great companies, they write, usually opt for a grand, audacious goal.

Boeing, for example, takes on challenges that would turn most corporate executives gray with fear. It literally bet the company, for example, on developing the 707 and 727. (The 727 was designed as a high-capacity jet that could land on short runways, such as those at New York's LaGuardia Airport.) If it hadn't succeeded in developing these planes once work began, the company might have gone under.

Most of you won't care to bet the company. But don't be timid. As Goethe said, "Boldness has genius and magic in it. Begin it now!"

Don't Water Down the Decision

Decisions usually benefit some in the organization and go against the wishes of others. If you choose to flood product idea A with resources and starve product B, B's in-house champions will be upset. They may work against the success of A.

Knowing that, you may be tempted to siphon off a few of A's resources to keep B limping along.

This is just what mediocre companies do. In trying to keep everyone happy, they don't capitalize fully on the opportunity at hand.

Another good example: politics. The reason there are so few landmark bills passed is that politicians try to please everyone, especially those whose votes they need. In the end, we get laws constructed of mud instead of crystal.

Go full force with your decision. In the end, events and the CEO may conspire to water it down, but at least you've begun as boldly and with as much strength as you can.

Analyze Forces

When you've made a decision and get ready to implement it, do a "force field" analysis. Take note of forces that will propel the decision toward success, and those that will hamper it.

Identify the forces that will work against your decision. Then figure out how to disarm each one.

For example, say you pick a new network server and operating system. Forces in your favor include the technology itself (because you picked the best); its in-house champions (who will enthusiastically introduce it); forward-thinking, early-adopting employees (who always want the latest and best tools to work with); and trainers from the software company (who will ease the transition).

Forces against may be employees who were in favor of a competing system; the technologically ill-at-ease, who will have trouble learning it; the go-it-slow crowd who never likes change of any kind; and the glitches you're sure are going to occur as you transition.

Once you've identified forces for and against, use that knowledge. Have a plan, for example, to neutralize the nay-sayers, to lavish training on the ill-at-ease, and to keep the system running when bugs strike.

Best Tip

Pilot tests often give you feedback you can use to improve the results of the full-blown rollout.

Do a Pilot Test

Whenever a consumer product company rolls out a new or reformulated product, it test markets it in a specific geographic location. If it sells in Duluth, it reasons, it'll work elsewhere.

A publishing company I worked for planned a line of low-priced cookbooks. It produced the first one and marketed it. If it succeeded, we'd do more. If it failed or barely broke even, we'd put our money elsewhere. It did so well that there are now twenty books in the series.

Pilot tests offer an added bonus: They often result in feedback you can use to strengthen a product or service.

You can also pilot-test programs that involve things other than products or services. You're thinking of changing over to a team structure? Start with a small test in one department or part of the plant. You wonder whether reengineering really works? Start with one process in a part of the company that always lags the industry.

Have a Contingency Plan

Whatever you decide, plan to stay on top of the decision and the indicators measuring its impact so you can abort or modify it if need be. And have a contingency plan.

Maybe it's your second choice. Say, for example, you decide to put more marketing money into advertising than in putting additional people on the road selling. Early indicators show that the new ads aren't working, so you stop running them and hire the new salespeople instead.

Implement the Decision with Power

Once you decide, go ahead with all your strength and heart. You need to show people you mean business, and you need to silence the critics. This is especially important if you're launching a product, restructuring, or introducing a new strategy.

I worked for a company that was entering a new business. It needed to show the staff that it not only intended to succeed but would do so quickly. Plus, it had to present its best face to the market. Thus, it had logos designed, stationery and business cards printed, and a variety of ads prepared long before introducing the product. It spared no expense in establishing a context for the business.

What if it hadn't done these things? The people working on the project might have wondered, "Do they really mean it? Are they hedging their bets? Maybe I should be worrying about what I'm going to do if this fails."

Put the Right People on the Job

Why do so many restructurings fail to produce the efficiency or profit gains its designers expect? Because, in part, the people implementing the decision don't fully believe in it. (And often with good reason!) They go about the job halfheartedly, which ensures failure.

With important decisions, halfhearted emotions and actions

are deadly. That's why you need to put the right people on the job—those who believe in what you're doing and why. Those who stand to gain something if they succeed. Those prepared to fight to the end to see the decision put into action.

These are the people who will make the decision work.

Pull the Plug Early

Steel baron Andrew Carnegie often encouraged his people to try new things—like process steel in innovative ways, find new ways to ship raw materials, or develop new work practices.

If things didn't work out, he pulled the plug on them quickly, even when a lot of money had been spent. He'd have workers throw up a building to house a new machine, for instance. If the machine didn't work out, he'd scrap the machine and the building both.

Charlie Chaplin operated the same way in making films. He'd explore plot lines, spending days filming them. Then, in an instant, he'd decide to change the story and begin filming a scene afresh.

You say resources are too expensive to work that way today and that more planning is necessary? Perhaps. But remember, genius has boldness in it . . .

With important decisions, put your most important, effective people on the job. They won't let you down.

Check Up Yourself

If you're intimately involved in a decision, be prepared to go out in the field to see that the decision is being carried out and that it's working. Don't say to yourself, "I have good people. They'll take care of it."

My brothers work in the construction industry. Every day, one or the other checks up on work in progress.

They often intervene in what's happening. They need to expedite part of the work, for example, or they discover that the job superintendent misunderstood instructions, that subcontractors are doing shoddy work, or that people are following the blueprint yet something doesn't feel quite right. Every day brings a new challenge, and they need to see with their own eyes how things are progressing.

Do the same when overseeing your decisions. Nobody cares as much as you do, and nobody will take as much responsibility.

The Agile Manager's Checklist

✔ Decisions on important things are rarely clear-cut. Expect the need for a few trade-offs and a little ambiguity.

✔ Keep a contingency plan in your back pocket just in case.

✔ Don't compromise at any stage of the decision-making process until the very end. Good, strong decisions rarely come out of committee work.

✔ Assess forces pro and con and use that knowledge to your advantage.

✔ If the decision looks like it's not going to work, cut your losses immediately.

Index